THE
REAL McCOY

THE REAL McCOY

and 149 Other Eponyms

Claire Cock-Starkey

Bodleian Library
UNIVERSITY OF OXFORD

First published in 2018 by the Bodleian Library
Broad Street, Oxford OX1 3BG
www.bodleianshop.co.uk

ISBN 978 1 85124 498 0

Text © Claire Cock-Starkey, 2018

Cover design by Dot Little at the Bodleian Library
Designed and typeset in Monotype Garamond
by illuminati, Grosmont
Printed and bound in China by C&C Offset Printing Co. Ltd
on 120 gsm Chinese Bajin

British Library Catalogue in Publishing Data
A CIP record of this publication is available from the British Library

INTRODUCTION

EPONYM *a person after whom a discovery, invention, place, etc., is named or thought to be named.*

As this definition from the *Oxford English Dictionary* attests, eponyms are usually adopted into common usage in celebration of a person's achievements, and as a result offer a fascinating story of discovery, innovation or inspiration.

Extraordinary figures from medicine, exploration and scientific research have thus lent their names to the English language, as can be witnessed, for example, in the eponyms Apgar score, Richter scale, Alzheimer's disease, foley artist, Angel Falls, Braille, Ferris wheel and diesel.

However, not all eponyms follow this traditional route into usage. Some don't actually reflect the original discoverer, but are named after an esteemed colleague or peer who perhaps deserved greater recognition; in this category we find Cadillac, Mount Everest, Mauritius, begonia and carpaccio.

Some individuals reach such heights of fame that their personal style is copied, leading to trendsetters such as Madame de Pompadour lending their names to the craze they began – in Pompadour's case the hairstyle she sported.

The cult of celebrity has also inspired chefs to develop new recipes for their famous patrons; for example, Dame Nellie Melba, the celebrated opera singer, had not one but two dishes created and named in her honour – peach Melba and Melba toast.

Looking further back in time, the mythology of ancient Rome and Greece has brought us yet more eponyms, weaving legends into our everyday language. Cereal, boreal, tantalize, panic and narcissism all derive from mythology. At times the legend itself reveals the meaning of the word – such as the self-loving Narcissus – but at other times the etymology is more obscure: the word panic, for example, comes from the hedonistic god Pan, whose booming yell inspired fear.

Literature and popular culture have also gifted us a number of characters with such strong associations that their names became words in their own right – into this category fall gargantuan, paparazzi and Svengali.

Naturally any investigation into the origin of a word attracts competing theories and disputes. A number of the eponyms featured within these pages have a muddied history, with the true individual celebrated in the naming of an object, location or concept lost in the mists of time. Eponyms thus disputed have been recognized and included here where there is an interesting story to tell, such as Béchamel sauce, Kalashnikov, Earl Grey tea, lynch and the real McCoy.

While having something named in your honour is generally a huge privilege, there are a small number of eponyms where the association is unwelcome, as in the case of guillotine, boycott and masochism. Some of my favourite eponyms are those that have been wrongly named, reflecting a fascinating tale of confusion, errors or, in some cases, just blatant credit stealing. These misnomers include salmonella, bloomers and America.

Science and medicine are especially littered with wrongly credited eponyms. In 1968 influential sociologist Robert K. Merton wrote a paper describing the 'Matthew Effect', after the parable of talents in the Gospel of Matthew, which suggested that senior colleagues often take the credit for their junior colleagues' discoveries. This theory was taken to its logical conclusion by a long-time correspondent and admirer of Merton, University of Chicago professor of statistics Stephen Stigler. When penning an essay in honour of Merton's retirement, Stigler (with tongue firmly in cheek) proposed Stigler's Law of Eponymy, which stated that 'No scientific discovery is named after its original discoverer' – the joke being that Stigler was taking Merton's own theory and naming it after himself. To further prove the very rule Stigler had highlighted, the 'new' law has since been adopted by the academic community and a number of papers and articles have been written about it.

This book includes 150 of the most fascinating origins of notable eponyms, revealing the stories behind some of our most intriguing words. Eponyms reflect characters from all walks of life – from royalty such as King Pyrrhus (who gave us pyrrhic victory) to criminals-turned-executioners like Thomas Derrick (who lent his name to the derrick crane) – and encompass history, science, literature, technology, medicine and the arts. In celebrating eponyms, then, we are also celebrating discovery, innovation, daring, trailblazing and infamy.

ALGORITHM *instructions/rules to follow in order to solve a calculation in a set number of steps, frequently used in computer programming*

Persian astronomer, scientist and mathematician Abdullah Muḥammad ibn Mūsā al-Khwārizmī (*c.* 780–*c.* 850) is known as the father of algebra because his systematic approach to quadratic equations laid the foundations for the discipline (and the word itself, *al-jabr*, comes from the title of his most famous work *Ḥisāb al-Jabr w'al-Muqābala*, *The Compendious Book on Calculation by Completion and Balancing*). When al-Khwārazmī's other noted book *On the Calculation with Hindu Numerals* was translated into Latin for a European audience in the twelfth century, his name was rendered as Algoritmi, which developed into the term 'algorithm'. Initially the term was used only in reference to the rules of performing arithmetic using Hindu–Arabic numerals, but by the mid-twentieth century it began to be associated with any method of problem solving, and, with the advent of mechanical computing, with computer programming.

ALZHEIMER'S DISEASE *the most common type of dementia*

Alois Alzheimer (1864–1915) was a doctor born in Marktbreit, Germany. He started his career working in hospitals in Frankfurt where he encountered 51-year-old Auguste Deter, a woman who showed progressive short-term memory loss. Alzheimer became fascinated by Deter and followed her case from 1901 until her death in 1906, when he was given permission to perform an autopsy. He noted that Deter's brain showed shrinkage in the cortex, neurofibrillary tangles and neuritic plaques – the first time that the pathology of a distinct type of dementia had been identified. The research carried out by Alzheimer proved vital in identifying and initiating our understanding of this complex disease and it is for this reason that by the 1970s his name was synonymous with the condition he first described in 1906.

AMAZON *a tall, strong woman*

In Greek mythology the Amazons were a tribe of female warriors who lived in a far-distant land. The myth developed from the persistent theme in the ancient world that there existed a place which was the opposite of traditional patriarchal society. The Amazons were said to be courageous warriors, rumoured to slice off one of their breasts to make using a bow and arrow easier. They maintained their female-only tribe by visiting nearby settlements to couple with the men, keeping any daughters but sending sons to live with their fathers. Many Greek heroes fought or fell in love with Amazon queens – Hercules fought Hippolyta, Achilles killed Penthesilea after falling in love with her during battle, and Theseus married Antiope. Numerous myths and legends built up around these warrior women, so that today when someone is described as Amazonian it summons up images of statuesque, powerful women. There are a number of competing theories on why the **AMAZON RIVER** got its name. The first suggests that it comes from a corruption of the Portuguese *amassona*, meaning boat-breaker, due to the tidal phenomenon in the lower Amazon which can cause sudden large waves. In a similar vein, some sources suggest it is a corruption of a Native American Tupi or Guarani word for 'big wave'. An alternative credits Spanish navigator Vicente Yáñez Pinzón (*c.*1460–1523), who accompanied Columbus on his first voyage to the New World in 1500. He was the first European to name the river, which he dubbed 'Rio Santa Maria de la Mar Dulce'. However, it was renamed the Amazon after the mythical warriors when, in 1541, explorer Francisco de Orellana sailed up the river and claimed to have been attacked by tribes of fierce female fighters.

AMERICA *the continents of North and South America*

The massive continents of North and South America are thought to have been named after one of the most controversial characters in the history of exploration, Amerigo Vespucci (1454–1512). Florentine navigator Vespucci claimed to have made four voyages to the New World (which in his writings he named *Mundus Novus*) in 1497, 1499, 1501 and 1503 – writing controversially in 1503 that he had reached the shores of Brazil in 1497, before Columbus. Vespucci's somewhat colourful (and at times factually dubious and vague) letters on his travels were widely translated and reproduced throughout Europe. Although his voyages are disputed, it does seem that he was one of the first to correctly identify the New World as a continent and not as the far reaches of Asia (which is how Columbus described it). More recently historians have expressed doubt that Vespucci reached Brazil as early as 1497 as the Spanish records do not support this. The cartographer Waldseemüller seemed to have doubts over the veracity of Vespucci's account as by 1513 he had removed the name 'America' from his map, but by then the name had stuck and has persisted. In recent years a rival theory has been put forward for the naming of America: the chief sponsor of John Cabot's 1497 expedition to Newfoundland was Richard ap Meryk (or Amerike) and some historians claim it was in his honour that the new land mass was named.

AMMONIA *a pungent, colourless inorganic gas; a compound of nitrogen and hydrogen*

Ammonia is named after the Egyptian god of life and reproduction, Amun (rendered as Ἄμμων, Ammon, by the Greeks). Large deposits of ammonium chloride were discovered by the Romans near the temple of Amun in Libya, which were probably formed from the dung of camels that were tethered outside the temple while their masters worshipped inside. When conquering North Africa the Romans used their usual tactic of adopting and assimilating local gods to their own deities; thus they renamed Amun as Jupiter Ammon, a ram-headed deity. As a result, the mineral which abounded at the temple became known as *sal ammoniacus*, sal ammoniac or 'salt of Ammon'. In 1782 the Swedish chemist Torbern Bergman discovered that you could derive the gas nitrogen hydride from sal ammoniac and so he named the gas 'ammonia' in recognition of its ancient roots. The fossilized cephalopod molluscs **AMMONITES** were also named after Ammon, due to their resemblance to the spiral curve of Jupiter Ammon's ram's horn.

AMPERE (AMP) *the current equal to a flow of 1 coulomb per second that 1 volt can send through a resistance of 1 ohm*

André-Marie Ampère (1775–1836) was a French scientist and mathematician who made many important discoveries in the burgeoning field of electromagnetism. As a child Ampère quickly revealed himself to be a true autodidact and was soon showing great promise as both a scientist and a mathematician. In 1814 he was accepted into the French Academy in Paris and in 1820 he went to watch Hans Christian Ørsted demonstrate his discovery that an electric current through a wire could disrupt a nearby magnetic needle, revealing the link between electricity and magnetism. Ampère became fascinated by electromagnetism and started his own research, soon making the discovery that parallel wires with currents travelling in the same direction will attract each other, and parallel wires with currents moving in the opposite directions will repel each other. This leap to create magnetic attraction without the use of magnets and by electricity alone was to be a giant step forwards in the field of electrodynamics. Ampère went on to formulate what came to be known as 'Ampère's Law', a complex mathematical equation which could connect the size of the magnetic field created to the electric current that produced it. This innovation is what Ampère is best remembered for, but he also advanced an early theory for the existence for electrons, discovered and named the element fluorine and created a precursor to the Periodic Table. Such was Ampère's influence that forty-five years after his death the International Electric Congress, in 1881, used his name to describe the SI unit for electric current, forever linking his name to the science of electricity.

ANGEL FALLS *the world's highest uninterrupted waterfall*

In 1933 James 'Jimmie' Crawford Angel (1899–1956) was flying over a remote jungle-covered area of Venezuela to prospect for gold when he came across the magnificent sight of the falls, plummeting 979 metres off the summit of the tabletop mountain Auyàntepui. When Angel returned to the USA he began telling people about the 'mile-high' waterfall he had seen, but many doubted his seemingly improbable story, which could not be proven as the area had yet to be properly mapped. Angel returned to the region in 1935 with two mining associates, Durand A. Hall and L.R. Dennison, and again later in the year with geologist Shorty Martin, who took the first photographs of the falls to verify the discovery. The news created great interest in the region and a number of expeditions were set up to explore the local geology, flora and fauna. In 1962 the region was protected as part of Canaima National Park. It has been disputed whether or not the falls were previously known to the indigenous Pemón tribe, as the falls were remote from their nearest village and Auyàntepui was avoided due to a belief that bad spirits haunted the area. However, it is clear that it was Jimmie Angel who brought the falls to the world's attention. After Angel's death his ashes were scattered over the falls in 1960, in recognition of his links to the natural wonder.

APGAR SCORE *a score 0–10 to assess the health of newborn babies*

The Apgar score was developed to assess quickly the health of newborn babies. Straight after birth a child is given a score based on five key indicators – skin colour, pulse rate, reflex, muscle tone and respiratory effort. A score of above 7 is normal, 4–6 is low and 0–3 is critically low. A baby with a low score generally requires medical attention; however, a low score is not always an indicator of future problems. The test was first developed in 1952 by Dr Virginia Apgar, an American obstetric anaesthetist. Apgar had become the first woman to be named a full professor at Columbia University College of Physicians and Surgeons in 1949, and her work in anaesthetics was trailblazing in an era when the field was only just being recognized among doctors. The score was initially developed to judge the effect on the baby of anaesthetics used during labour, but its usefulness as a general guide to newborn health was soon noted. After Apgar published details of the scheme in 1953, it soon became standard the world over and continues to be widely used today.

APHRODISIAC *a foodstuff, drink or drug which excites sexual desire*

The word 'aphrodisiac' first came into the English language in the early eighteenth century from the Greek ἀφροδισιακόν, *aphrodisiakon*, which means pertaining to Aphrodite, the goddess of love. There are a number of myths surrounding the birth of Aphrodite. The best known tells that she rose out of the sea foam aboard a giant scallop shell after Cronus castrated his father Uranus and threw his severed genitals into the sea. Aphrodite was very beautiful and wore a special girdle in which she kept magical enchantments which caused men to desire her. In Greek mythology the outbreak of the Trojan War can be traced back to Aphrodite. During a celebratory banquet, Eris produced a golden apple from the Garden of Hesperides, which she asked Zeus to gift to the most beautiful guest. Aphrodite, Hera and Athena all nominated themselves for the honour. Not wanting to cause discord, Zeus refused to judge, instead asking the mortal Paris to decide. Each goddess offered Paris a gift in return for choosing her, with Aphrodite offering him the hand of Helen of Sparta. Paris immediately selected Aphrodite as the winner. It was the Greeks' mission to retrieve Helen from Paris in Troy which precipitated the Trojan War.

ASPERGER'S SYNDROME *a high-functioning subgroup of autism*

Hans Asperger (1906–1980) was an Austrian paediatrician who noticed that four of his patients displayed remarkably similar personality traits, and extrapolated that they might have the same condition. The four boys were all socially awkward, clumsy, lacked empathy and yet demonstrated an intense interest in a chosen subject, about which they could talk eloquently and at length. Asperger published his findings in 1947 and dubbed the condition 'autistic psychopathy'. He wrote about the condition in a positive way, noting that he believed these 'little professors' could go on to great things as adults, an attitude which at the time was enlightened. Asperger's work, written in German, gained little traction until British researcher Lorna Wing published a paper using the term 'Asperger's syndrome' in 1981 and recognition of the condition grew. The story took a disturbing turn in 2018, when medical historian Herwig Czech published a paper claiming that Asperger had collaborated with the Nazi party and may have referred some children to the Am Spiegelgrund clinic in Vienna, where child euthanasia was carried out.

AXEL *a figure-skating jump in which the skater takes off from the outer edge of one skate, performs one and a half turns and lands on the rear outside edge of the other skate*

In 1882 at what is now considered the first ever international figure-skating competition, the Great International Skating Tournament in Vienna, Norwegian skater Axel Paulsen (1855–1938) first performed an innovative new jump. Paulsen was a classic Norwegian skater; he competed as both a speed skater and a figure skater and it was his power and pace which marked him out. In the 1880s the Viennese style of skating was dominant, characterized by intricate footwork, but Paulsen burst onto the scene skating in the Nordic style using high speeds and powerful jumps. At the 1882 tournament Paulsen won gold in the speed skating and came third in the figure skating after debuting his impressive new jump (made all the more impressive as he competed in speed skates as opposed to figure skates). Paulsen's new jump was recognized in a prize for 'best special figure' and has since gone on to be perfected and improved by subsequent skaters – in 1978 Vern Taylor of Canada became the first person to successfully land a triple axel in competition. Paulsen continued to compete throughout the 1880s and was hugely successful as a speed skater, holding the speed skating world title from 1882 to 1890 and introducing the technique whereby speed skaters race with their hands clasped behind their backs.

BAFFIN ISLAND *Canadian island, fifth largest in the world*

Baffin Island, situated in the Arctic north of Canada, is the fifth largest island in the world. Although Baffin Island has been continuously inhabited by Inuit for centuries, historians think it likely that it was also known to the Vikings by 1000 CE because it is thought to have been referred to as Helluland ('stone-slab land') in Icelandic sagas. The island was 'officially' discovered by Europeans in 1576 when British explorer Martin Frobisher landed there during his mission to discover the Northwest Passage. By 1616 William Baffin (1584–1622), on another Northwest Passage expedition, had charted what became known as **FROBISHER BAY**. After concluding that the island was not a gateway to the passage to India, he proceeded to name the island and bay after himself, and a number of its geographical features after his esteemed colleagues.

BAKELITE *the first thermosetting plastic*

Bakelite was the first fully synthetic plastic, marking a great leap forwards for the cheap manufacture of goods. It was developed by Belgian scientist Leo Baekeland (1863–1944) in 1907 after he began researching alternatives to natural shellac, which was made from the shells of the Asian lac beetle. While working in New York, Baekeland discovered that if he heated and exerted great pressure on a mix of phenol and formaldehyde it created a hard-setting synthetic plastic, which could be put to many uses. Baekeland announced his invention publicly in 1909 and went on to form General Bakelite in 1911, a commercial company based in New Jersey. Bakelite became a huge commercial success, being used both industrially in radios and car manufacture and later around the home as brightly coloured telephones, ashtrays and jewellery. Prior to the invention of Bakelite the most commonly used plastic was celluloid, which was highly flammable and easily dissolved. Thus the innovation of Bakelite, which was strong, durable and infusible, caused a boom in synthetic plastics and led the way for many future innovations in this field.

BASKERVILLE   *a serif typeface*

John Baskerville (1706–1775) came late to the book business, turning his hand to typesetting at the age of fifty having made his fortune in japanned wares. Baskerville was an innovator, becoming one of the first British typographers to oversee a book for its entire production – from designing and cutting the type to selecting the paper and developing the ink. Baskerville was extremely fastidious and put a great deal of time into designing the most beautifully typeset books. As a result his work rarely made any money and yet was highly prized for its quality and clarity. Baskerville designed his eponymous typeface in 1757, creating a crisp, open serif font. The typeface became especially famous due to Baskerville using it in his celebrated printings of the

Bible for Cambridge University Press in 1763. The Baskerville typeface spread to America after Benjamin Franklin met Baskerville and took a sample of his type back with him, where it was used for printing US federal government papers. After his death Baskerville's punches and matrices were sold to a French firm, ensuring the typeface was widely used across Europe, until superseded by the development of more modern fonts. Baskerville has enjoyed a resurgence of late, its legibility ensuring it has remained a popular typeface, especially for book printing.

BÉCHAMEL SAUCE *a white sauce made with milk, flour and butter*

In an era before refrigeration, keeping meat and fish fresh was difficult. One solution to this was to use a strongly flavoured sauce to mask the potentially putrid taste of meat past its best. As a consequence, white sauce made with butter, flour and milk is seen widely in both Italian and French cooking. Milk was hard to keep fresh before refrigeration and so any sauce made with milk or cream was perceived as the preserve of the rich. A number of stories have been put forward for the origin of béchamel sauce, from the Italian cooks at the court of the French queen Catherine de' Medici to the inveterate sauce creator Duke Philippe de Mornay (who was also responsible for **MORNAY SAUCE**, a variant of béchamel including cheese). However, most historians agree that it was named in honour of Marquis Louis de Béchamel (d.1703). Béchamel was a financier and held the post of chief steward of King Louis XIV; it thus seems unlikely he created the sauce himself. Instead, it seems that renowned chef and leading proponent of haute cuisine François Pierre de la Varenne (1615–1678) probably improved on an existing sauce and dedicated it to Béchamel.

BEGONIA *a genus of subtropical and tropical brightly coloured flowering plants*

The begonia was named after botanist Michel Bégon (1638–1710) during a plant-collecting trip to the Caribbean in 1690 – one of the first instances of a plant being named in honour of a fellow botanist, starting something of a trend. Bégon was governor of the important French seaport Rochefort, from where boats set off on voyages of discovery, and it was Bégon who transformed this small port into a major maritime centre. As the New World opened up, King Louis XIV instructed Bégon to organize an expedition to search for new and exotic plants in the French-controlled Caribbean islands of Martinique and Santo Domingo (modern-day Haiti). Monk and botanist Charles Plumier was employed aboard the ship to collect and document new plants, and it was he who identified and named the begonia in honour of his patron. Plumier was so successful at identifying new species that he was named King's Botanist and was sent on a number of further voyages, during which he collected over 1,000 new plant species. In 1753 Carl Linnaeus used 'begonia' in his influential book on plant taxonomy, *Species Plantarum*, and the name was fixed. The first begonia to reach Europe alive went to Kew Gardens in 1777, which inspired the cultivation and popularity of the species in Europe. In 1986 the city of Rochefort was able to acquire the outstanding begonia collection of breeder Vincent Millerioux. The

Conservatory of Begonias was built to house the collection, which features over 200 varieties and provides a space for botanists to study the plants in the city that their namesake made great.

BERING STRAIT *the body of water that separates Asia and North America*

Danish explorer Vitus Bering (1681–1741) was a member of the Russian fleet of Tsar Peter the Great. In 1724 Peter's widow, Catherine the Great, tasked Bering to discover if Asia and North America were connected by land. By August 1728 Bering had sailed through the then unnamed Bering Strait into the Arctic Ocean, proving that the two land masses were not attached. This had been no mean feat: Bering left St Petersburg in 1725, travelling across the largely unexplored expanse of Siberia, suffering food shortages and incredibly harsh winters; he and his team and their equipment reached Kamchatka on the Siberian peninsula early in 1728. Before they could set sail, Bering and his team had to build their boat, which was at last ready by July. After successfully identifying the strait, it took Bering another two years to journey back to St Petersburg. In 1741 Bering once again set sail from Kamchatka in order to expand on his findings, discovering a number of islands in the Aleutian chain and spotting Mount Saint Elias in Alaska. Unfortunately by this time the crew were ravaged by scurvy. Bering's ship the *St Peter* became shipwrecked on what later became known as Bering Island, and the crew sought shelter ashore. Unfortunately the island was almost completely barren, with no trees to provide shelter, so the scurvy-ridden sailors took refuge in ravines and many died, including Bering. Forty-five of the *St Peter*'s 75-man crew survived the wreck and the long winter on Bering Island before fashioning a boat and finally returning home, ensuring that the discoveries of Bering's last expedition were not lost. In recognition of Bering's legacy the Bering Strait, Bering Sea, Bering Island and Bering Glacier are all named after him.

BERMUDA *archipelago in the North Atlantic*

Bermuda was first spotted by a European in *c.*1505 when the Spanish ship *La Garza*, captained by Juan de Bermúdez (d.1570), sailed past on its journey from Cadiz to Mexico. Bermúdez reportedly again passed the isle in 1509, when he thoughtfully deposited a number of pigs there in order to feed any unfortunate sailors who might get washed up after a shipwreck. In 1511 'La Bermuda' was labelled on a map for the first time when Spanish map-maker Peter Martyr d'Anghiera published his book of Spanish discoveries in the Caribbean. The island remained uninhabited until 1609, though it did play temporary host to a number of shipwreck survivors. Habitation commenced after the *Sea Venture*, captained by Sir George Somers, which had set sail from England bound for the new settlement of Jamestown in Virginia, was wrecked off Bermuda and the 150 sailors and settlers took refuge on the island. After ten months they had fashioned two new boats and finally sailed on to Jamestown. They did, however, leave three men behind, and it was they who ensured the continued settlement of Bermuda and secured Britain's claim on the land.

BERSERK *acting in an out-of-control manner*

The word 'berserk' derives from the ancient Norse berserkers – warriors who fought furiously and uncontrollably. Berserkers wore the pelts of bears as cloaks and in Norse sagas were portrayed as having almost superhuman fighting power, entering battle in a trance-like state – howling like wolves, gnashing their teeth and terrifying all who faced them. It has been suggested that the berserkers used drugs or alcohol to create their frenzied state, but other historians maintain that they worked themselves up into a state of hysteria in order to enter battle without fear. Whatever the reason for their wild and indiscriminate fighting style, the berserkers were outlawed in 1015 by the Icelandic law code and soon after disbanded. The word crept into English, named after the Norse warriors, from 1814 when Sir Walter Scott utilized it in his writing.

BIRO *ballpoint pen*

Hungarian László Bíró (1899–1985) was a newspaper editor who became fed up with fountain pens smudging and spilling ink on the page when he was making notes. He noticed that newspaper ink was much quicker to dry and yet was too thick to flow from a fountain pen. Bíró realized a new pen technology was needed. He began working with his brother György and machinist Andor Goy to develop a workable ballpoint pen. The idea had been patented by John Loud in the late nineteenth century, but his design did not work on paper and was used only for marking leather. By 1931 Bíró had developed a prototype pen, which he showed at the Budapest World Fair. The situation in Europe was becoming tense as war loomed, and by 1938 Hungary was allied with Nazi Germany. As a Jew, Bíró faced persecution so he and his brother fled to Paris and then Madrid. Argentine president Augustín Justo was impressed with Bíró's prototype product and invited him to Argentina to manufacture the pens there, securing an Argentine patent in 1943. During the Second World War the RAF ordered thousands of the new ballpoint pens from Bíró to use at high altitude, as unlike fountain pens they did not leak. In 1950 Bíró sold his patent to Frenchman Marcel Bich, who improved the design and gave them the name Bic Cristal. This pen revolutionized the market as it was reliable and cheap. However, the early association with its inventor did not fade in Britain and the name 'biro' stuck as a generic term for plastic ballpoint pens.

BLOOMERS *baggy trousers cinched at the ankle and worn under a skirt*

In 1850s' America a new women's movement was on the rise, taking issue with the impractical nature of women's dress. During this period women generally wore long dresses which dragged in the mud, and heavily boned corsets which played havoc with their internal organs. Elizabeth Smith Miller of New York began wearing an innovative new outfit inspired by traditional Turkish costume: a shorter dress over loose trousers fastened at the ankle. Amelia Jenks Bloomer, a fellow women's rights activist and editor of the temperance journal *The Lily*, was inspired by Miller and took to wearing the 'reform dress', as it became known. As Bloomer garnered more attention for her outlandish outfit, it became associated with her name, being referred to as the 'Bloomer costume'. Women all over America were keen to throw off their long and heavy skirts which impinged on their ability to move freely and carry out physical tasks – clothes, therefore, came to be seen as another way in which women were held back in society. The growing tide of women adopting bloomers was not without controversy, with some opponents claiming the outfit was indecent. Leading advocates of women's rights Susan B. Anthony, Elizabeth Cady Stanton and Lucy Stone all began sporting bloomers, and the outfit became linked with calls for women's suffrage. Unfortunately the press coverage of the scandalous 'bloomers' soon began to overshadow their message of reform and many activists reluctantly returned to wearing more traditional long skirts to refocus attention on their cause.

BLURB *short punchy promotional description of a book, film or other product*

American humorist Gelett Burgess (1866–1951) is the originator of this literary eponym. In 1907 Burgess was promoting his book *Are You a Bromide?* and, as was customary at the time, he had 500 promotional copies printed to give out at the American Booksellers Association banquet. For maximum impact Burgess designed a special dust jacket on which was printed the picture of a glamorous woman (taken from a dental magazine), whom he named Miss Belinda Blurb, shouting out fulsome praise for his book. Though it was intended as a parody, the 'blurb' was so successful that it soon caught on with other publishers and has today become the norm.

BOBBY *nickname for a British police officer*

The Metropolitan Police was founded by British home secretary Sir Robert Peel (1788–1850) in 1829. It was the first professional police force in London, replacing the rather rag-tag system of nightwatchmen, soldiers and local constables who had hitherto been in charge of law and order. Peel's new policemen, in their tall hats and dark blue jackets, became a familiar sight in London, walking the beat to provide visual reassurance to citizens. Because of their association with the politician who founded the force, they colloquially became known as 'peelers' or, more permanently, 'bobbies' after the nickname for Robert. The first bobbies worked seven days a week for £1 and received only five unpaid days of holiday a year. They were not allowed to vote and had to gain permission to get married.

BODLEIAN, THE *Oxford University library*

Thomas Bodley (1545–1613) was an Oxford graduate and diplomat who worked for Elizabeth I. In 1598, when retired, he decided to invest his fortune in refounding Oxford University library, which had been decimated during the Reformation, and by 1602 the beautiful Duke Humfrey's Library was reopened with over 2,000 books. Bodley was passionate about his library and set up numerous systems, with stipulations to ensure it was well run and continued to grow – including introduction of the 'no lending' rule that prevented books going astray; the condition that 'no fire or flame' should be kindled in the library, ensuring the precious collection remained safe; and establishing a precursor to legal deposit which meant a copy of every book published in

England was deposited at the library. The refounded library was named in Bodley's honour. Today it is a world-renowned institution and the second largest library in Britain.

BOLIVIA *country in South America*

Bolivia takes its name from the great South American revolutionary Simón Bolívar (1783–1830), who helped to liberate numerous countries in South America from Spanish control. Bolívar was born in Venezuela to a wealthy Creole family but was sent to Europe for his education, where he became impassioned by the ideas of Enlightenment thinkers such as Rousseau and Voltaire. As a young adult Bolívar returned to Venezuela determined that South American states should fight for independence from Spanish colonial rule, and from 1808 he campaigned and fought for a free Venezuela, which was achieved in 1821. Bolívar continued to fight Spanish rule and helped found Gran Colombia (formed from modern-day Colombia, Venezuela, Ecuador, Panama and parts of Brazil, Peru and Guyana), serving as its president from 1819 to 1830, and ousted the Spanish from Peru, Ecuador and Bolivia (which was then named in his honour). As a great hero of the independence of South America, Bolívar is honoured not just in the naming of Bolivia but also in numerous Plaza Bolívars across the region and in the currencies of Bolivia (the **BOLIVIANO**) and Venezuela (the **BOLIVAR**).

BOREAL *of the north*

This word came into English usage in the fifteenth century from the Latin *borealis*, which itself stems from Boreas

– the Greek god of the north wind. Boreas was one of the Ancient Greek Ἄνεμοι, Anemoi, the four wind gods, the others being Zephyrus (west wind), Notus (south wind) and Eurus (east wind). Boreas was pictured as a winged man, bringing in winter with his breath of cold north wind. Greek folklore tells that in the spring Zephyr and Boreas would blow through fields of mares, impregnating them as wind stallions. It was said that the horses born from the Anemoi were the fastest and best of all horses.

BOYCOTT *protesting by refusing to engage commercially or otherwise with a company, political party or person with whom you disagree*

Unusually for many eponyms, this word's origin can be traced to a precise year: 1880, during the Irish Land War. At this time the Irish Land League was working to protect workers' rights against landlords who charged unfair rents to their tenant farmers. These relatively powerless people were encouraged to stop engaging with the land agent representing their wealthy landlords, ostracizing them from their local community, in what became an effective non-violent form of protest. The word 'boycott' comes from the victim of one of these early protests, a retired army captain and land agent in County Mayo, Charles C. Boycott (1832–1897). When it looked likely that crops would fail, precipitating a famine, Boycott's tenants asked him to reduce rents by 25 per cent. Boycott refused and attempted to evict his unruly tenants. The Land League encouraged them to shun Boycott and refuse to communicate with anyone associated with him. Although their efforts were ultimately futile, as Boycott simply employed harvesters from elsewhere, the media coverage of the case soon led to the creation of the eponymous word, and so the use of this political tactic, and thus the word, spread. The *Oxford English Dictionary* notes that not only did the word quickly achieve common usage in the English language but it was also soon adopted in French (*boycotter*), German (*boycottieren*) and Russian (*Бойкотировать*) among others.

BOYSENBERRY *a hybrid berry from blackberries, raspberries and loganberries*

In 1920s' California, horticulturalist Rudolph Boysen (1895–1950) experimented with crossing a number of berries to create a hybrid aggregate fruit. The fruits of Boysen's labours quite literally paid off when he successfully crossed loganberries, blackberries and raspberries to produce a new, large, deep-red berry. Despite the flavoursome nature of the berry, Boysen was unable to make it a commercial success, and after breaking his back in an accident he reluctantly sold his farm. In 1927 fellow horticulturalist and berry expert Walter Knott heard of Boysen's experimental new berry and was intrigued. Knott tracked down Boysen's old farm and discovered there a number of withered vines, which he transported back to his farm and nursed back to health. After much love and attention the vines began to bear fruit and Knott was delighted to find the resultant berry delicious. Knott went on to cultivate the hybrid, naming it 'boysenberry' in honour of its developer, and soon it gained widespread popularity across California. Today boysen-berries are used in jams, pies and preserves. New Zealand is now the world's largest boysenberry grower.

BRAILLE *tactile reading and writing system for the blind*

Louis Braille (1809–1852) was born in Coupvray, France. At the age of three he injured his eye while playing with an awl in his father's workshop. Unfortunately the eye became infected; the infection soon spread to the other eye, leaving Louis completely blind. He began attending the National Institute for Blind Youth in Paris. Impatient to learn, he became preoccupied with developing a better system for the blind to read. At that time the only method was to trace embossed letters, but this involved learning all the letter shapes by feel, which was fiendishly difficult and painfully slow. A breakthrough came in 1821, when a former soldier, Charles Barbier, visited the school to demonstrate a system of raised dots and dashes he called night writing. Barbier's system helped illiterate soldiers send and receive messages without striking a light and revealing their location. Louis was inspired by Barbier's idea and began to develop and simplify the system into a code. By 1824 fifteen-year-old Louis had refined it to just six dots to represent the entire alphabet. Louis continued to develop Braille, ultimately perfecting a code of 63 characters, made up of one to six raised dots, arranged in a matrix in one of six positions, which allows blind people to read by lightly passing their finger over the text. The system was officially adopted at Braille's school in 1854, two years after his death, but was not popularized internationally until 1932 when an official Braille code for the English-speaking world was agreed. Today Braille is widely used across the world and continues to be refined and updated.

BRONX, THE *one of the five boroughs of New York*

Jonas Bronck (1600–1643) was born in Sävsjö, Sweden, later emigrating to Denmark, then to the Netherlands. After 1639, when the tulip-mania bubble burst and the economy drooped, Bronck and his wife set sail for New Amsterdam (New York today). The couple bought some land and built a house overlooking the Harlem River, hoping to farm tobacco. Their farm grew to 680 acres and took in the banks of the Aquahung, which came to be known as Bronck's River. Jonas Bronck died childless aged forty-three of an unknown ailment (some historians posit that he was killed by Native Americans in retaliation for the Dutch-instigated Pavonia Massacre). His wife remarried and moved away. Bronck's name, however, lived on in Bronck's River, which over the years became rendered as Bronx, and went on to inspire the name for the entire borough.

BUDDLEIA *a shrub with lilac, white or golden flowers, popular with butterflies and insects*

The father of modern taxonomy Carl Linnaeus was responsible for naming the buddleia (also rendered as buddleja) in 1753 after English botanist the Reverend Adam Buddle (1662–1715). Adam Buddle was one of the first English botanists to specialize in mosses and liverworts. He was especially interested in the theory of plant classification, which at that time was in its infancy. Buddle created a herbarium, which today is part of the Sloane herbarium at the Natural History Museum, and poured his life's knowledge into a book entitled *English Flora*, which was completed in 1708 but never published; it survives in the Sloane manuscript collection at the British Library. It was this manuscript which brought Buddle to the attention of Linnaeus, who was so impressed by his knowledge that he decided to name a whole genus – the *Buddleia* – after him. The first buddleia to come to Britain was the golden-flowered *Buddleia globosa*, which arrived from Chile in 1774. Soon, further varieties arrived from all over Asia, the plant's beautiful butterfly-attracting flowers and hardy character making it a staple of English gardens. The most popular buddleia today is the *Buddleia davidii*, which was named in honour of its discoverer Père Armand David (1826–1900). David was a Lazarist missionary from the French Pyrenees who brought back numerous specimens of plants and animals from his expeditions to China, including the buddleia that now bears his name and a giant-panda skin.

BUNSEN BURNER *burner used in chemistry labs with a clean, almost colourless flame*

Robert Bunsen (1811–1899) was a German chemist who, over the course of a long career in which he made many important discoveries, developed one of the foundation pieces of modern laboratory equipment, the Bunsen burner. In 1834 Bunsen published his discovery, alongside physician Arnold Berthold, of iron oxide hydrate as an antidote to arsenic poisoning. This proved especially prescient as in 1843 he lost the sight in his right eye after some arsenic exploded in his face, resulting in serious arsenic poisoning, which was cured by his own antidote. Chemists had long identified various elements by sprinkling a sample into a flame and observing what colour it burned; however, the natural colour of the flame could cause a misreading. As a consequence, Bunsen and his laboratory assistant Peter Desaga developed a burner which introduced air into the gas in a controlled fashion, allowing the creation of an almost colourless, soot-free flame. This innovation greatly assisted Bunsen and his colleague Gustav Kirchhoff in their experiments with spectroscopy – the analysis of the light emitted by burning elements when diffused through a prism – and helped them to identify two new elements, caesium and rubidium.

CADILLAC *American luxury car brand*

Cadillac is one of America's oldest car firms, established in 1902 in Detroit, Michigan. The company was named after French explorer Antoine Laumet de la Mothe, sieur de Cadillac (1658–1730), who founded the city of Detroit. Cadillac joined the French army as a young man and was posted to Port Royal in New France (today Annapolis, Nova Scotia, Canada) in 1683. Cadillac was something of an expert navigator and soon became an important part of the local administration in New France. In 1698 Cadillac travelled back to France to ask King Louis XIV for permission to found a new French settlement lower in the Great Lakes region, south of Lake Huron, near an area known as *le détroit*, or the straits. Cadillac secured permission and the settlement was officially created in 1701 with the name Fort Ponchartrain du Detroit, which soon became shortened to Detroit. The explorer's impact on the region can also be seen in the naming of the city of Cadillac in Michigan and Cadillac Mountain in Maine.

CARDIGAN *button-up knitted sweater*

The cardigan is named after James Thomas Brudenell, the 7th Earl of Cardigan (1797–1868), after he reportedly wore the garment during the Crimean War. Brudenell was by all accounts a quick-tempered, spoilt character who rose through the military ranks by repeatedly paying for promotion. His behaviour was frequently unsavoury – he ran off with another man's wife, wounded a man in a duel and had an underling arrested for placing wine on the table in a black bottle instead of a decanter; however, his status and wealth ensured he went largely unchallenged. With dashing good looks, Brudenell cared about appearances; he spent £10,000 a year kitting out his regiment, the 11th Hussars, ensuring they were the best-turned-out soldiers. Cardigan became a hero in 1854 during the Crimean War when he led his troops in the ill-conceived Charge of the Light Brigade at Balaclava. Brudenell was reportedly the first onto the field, charging up to the Russian guns (and then quickly turning round in order to exit the field unscathed); it is said that it was during this foray that he sported the knitted, fur-trimmed jacket to which he later lent his name. Other historians argue that it was his troops who wore the knitted garment to keep out the Crimean cold, and accounts differ as to whether it was a sleeveless knitted waistcoat or a knitted jacket. Whatever the form of the cardigan, it gained notice when Brudenell returned to Britain and was fêted by the press, inspiring the widespread popularity of the knitted buttoned-up sweater and permanently linking his name to its many guises. The Crimean War gifted us with two further sartorial words: the **BALACLAVA** – a knitted hat covering the entire face with holes for eyes and mouth, named after the Battle of

Balaclava; and **RAGLAN SLEEVES** – a design of sleeve which extends all the way to the collar, named after Lord Raglan, a British general who had lost his arm at Waterloo and required a less restrictive style of sleeve.

CARPACCIO *thinly sliced raw beef, served with a vinaigrette*

The original beef carpaccio was invented in 1950 by Giuseppe Cipriani, owner of Harry's Bar in Venice. According to Cipriani's memoir, the appetizer was created for Countess Amalia Nani Mocenigo, whose doctors had advised she should avoid cooked meat. Cipriani claimed to have named the dish after the Italian Renaissance artist Vittore Carpaccio (*c.*1465–1520), who was renowned for using in his paintings a red pigment which resembled raw meat. Cipriani was clearly a fan of Renaissance art as he also named the cocktail invented at his establishment a **BELLINI**, after Venetian painter Giovanni Bellini (1430–1516).

CASANOVA *a charming but feckless womanizer*

Giacomo Girolamo Casanova (1725–1798) was an Enlightenment-era polymath, originally from Venice, who travelled widely across Europe. Casanova came to fame (or, rather, infamy) due to his gloriously salacious memoirs *Story of My Life*, which he wrote while eking out his old age as a librarian in Castle Dux, Bohemia. The memoirs contain countless tales of his sexual prowess and detail over 120 dalliances with women from all sections of society, from milkmaids to nuns – and it is for this reason that his name came to be used for a great lover. While it is true that his conquests were many, his memoirs reveal that his life was full of excitement and interest. He rubbed shoulders with Voltaire, Catherine the Great and Benjamin Franklin; he evaded arrest, took part in duels and broke out of prison. Casanova's memoirs were first published in 1822 in Germany, but the manuscript was deemed so scandalous that it was heavily redacted and edited; even so, it was widely printed across Europe, and by 1888 the term 'Casanova' had crept into usage, showing that even the toned-down version was fairly racy. The full, unedited version of Casanova's memoirs was not published until 1960 in the original French. It remains one of the most fascinating and candid Enlightenment-era memoirs to have survived.

CELSIUS *temperature scale based on the boiling and freezing points of water*

Swedish astronomer Anders Celsius (1701–1744) developed his temperature scale in 1742, based on the freezing and boiling points of water. His original scale was the inversion of today's scale, with 0 representing the boiling point of water and 100 the freezing point. It was reversed in 1745 by Carl Linnaeus and it is this version which has persisted. The scale is also known as 'centigrade' as it is divided into a hundred degrees. For many years Celsius's scale was referred to as the Swedish thermometer, but in 1948 it was finally given his name as an official measurement at an international conference on weights and measures (Conférence générale des poids et mesures). Today most countries in the world use Celsius to measure temperature; an exception is America, where Daniel Gabriel Fahrenheit's scale (see page 48), which was developed in 1724, becoming the first standardized temperature scale, has remained dominant.

CEREAL *food grains such as oats, corn, wheat and rye*

This word came into use in the nineteenth century to describe grains that are used for food, but it originates in the Latin word *cerealis*, which is derived from associations with Ceres, the Roman goddess of agriculture. Ceres was a benevolent goddess, the daughter of Saturn and Ops; she was believed to have given humans the gift to cultivate corn and brought fertility to the land. She is often pictured with a farm tool in one hand and a basket of fruit, grains or flowers in the other. The Romans explained the ebb and flow of the seasons through a myth related to Ceres. Ceres' daughter Proserpina was taken into the underworld after lonely Pluto, god of the underworld, fell in love with her having been hit with one of Cupid's arrows. Ceres was devastated to lose her daughter and plunged the world into famine, so Jupiter sent Mercury into the underworld to ask Pluto to return Proserpina to earth. Unfortunately while in the underworld Proserpina had eaten six pomegranate seeds – the fruit of the dead – and as a consequence she could not remain in the world of the living. Proserpina was allowed out of the underworld each spring and Ceres would celebrate by making the plants burst into life. Proserpina and Ceres would spend the summer happily together and plants would flourish, before Ceres would begin to grow unhappy at her daughter's imminent return to the underworld, heralding the arrival of autumn. Proserpina was forced to spend the winter months back in the underworld with Pluto, and so in the world of the living nothing would grow while Ceres sadly waited for her return.

CHAUVINIST *a person who shows prejudiced fervour for their own cause, sex or country*

Since the 1960s chauvinism has been mainly associated with sexism, but prior to this it was more akin to overt patriotism and exaggerated nationalism. The word came into usage in the 1840s with this meaning, after a semi-mythical French soldier, Nicolas Chauvin. The character of Chauvin was stereotyped in a number of plays, including the popular 1831 vaudeville *La Cocarde Tricolore* by the Cogniard brothers, but historians are unclear as to whether Chauvin was ever once a real person or pure fiction. The character Chauvin was a French soldier who fought successfully in Napoleon's army, eventually receiving a pension and medals for his good service. After the tide had turned against Napoleon and he was exiled to St Helena, Chauvin continued to blindly worship his old leader. It was this ill-advised fervent patriotism which was sent up in the character of Chauvin, and it is for this reason that his name seeped into first the French and then the English language. Today the word can be used with any number of modifiers, such as male or human, to indicate in what sphere the superiority is thought to derive.

CHESTERFIELD *a deep-buttoned leather-covered sofa*

The chesterfield sofa, with its characteristic arms and back of the same height, adorned with deep-set buttons and a leather covering, has become a British design icon, but its origins are not clear-cut. It has been said that the sofa is named after Lord Philip Stanhope, the 4th Earl of Chesterfield (1694–1773), a prominent diplomat, wit and arbiter of taste. Stanhope was said to have commissioned a sofa of a similar design in the mid-eighteenth century, specifying that it must allow gentlemen to sit upright with dignity, without getting their clothes rumpled. It is thought this was where the design for the low-slung sofa derived; however, the button-tufting and deep-sprung seat were likely later additions as these innovations were not developed until the nineteenth century. One apocryphal story of the sofa's origins comes from Stanhope's deathbed. Mr Dayrolles, a budding diplomat and godson of Stanhope, went to pay his respects to his dying godfather; as he was ushered into the room Stanhope urged the servant, with his dying breath, to 'Give Mr Dayrolles a chair'. The servant, unsure of his master's meaning, instead of offering Dayrolles a seat handed over the sofa. Dayrolles hefted the unwieldy piece of furniture home, where it became much admired and frequently copied, ensuring its place in many British sitting rooms.

COLOMBIA *republic in north-west South America*

Colombia is the only country in the Americas that has re-tained the name which celebrates the discoverer of America, Christopher Columbus (1451–1506). Born Cristoforo Colombo in Genoa, he forged a career as a sailor, soon becoming motivated by the desire to seek a new westward passage to Asia (or the Indies as he called it). After searching for backing in both Spain and Portugal he finally secured a sponsor in the shape of King Ferdinand and Queen

Isabella of Spain; in August 1492 he set sail with his fleet of three ships, the *Santa María*, the *Pinta* and the *Niña*. On 12 October 1492 Columbus and his men set foot on land (an island which is now part of the Bahamas), believing they had reached the Orient and thus greeting the natives as 'Indians', a misnomer which was to stick. Columbus explored a few other islands in the Indies before sailing back to Spain amid much fanfare. Discussions over whether this truly was the Orient, or in fact a New World, raged but Columbus himself was adamant he had discovered a shorter route to Asia. He later led two further voyages to the Indies, maintaining his belief. Despite his geographical confusion, Columbus has been credited with opening up the New World for European settlement (which in the process devastated the native populations). The modern country of Colombia was 'discovered' by Europeans in 1499 and was conquered by Rodrigo de Bastidas in 1525 when he established the settlement of Santa Maria, ushering in a brutal era of Spanish colonization. Independence from Spain was won in 1819, led by Simón Bolívar (see page 24); the Republic of Colombia was declared in 1886.

COLT *a type of revolver*

That the name Colt has become synonymous with a revolver is testament to the invention and self-promotion of Samuel Colt (1814–1862). As a young man Colt spent time at sea training to be a navigator, sailing for a year aboard the *Corvo* in 1830. It is said that his idea for a gun with a revolving chamber, meaning it could shoot multiple rounds before needing to be reloaded, was inspired by observing the ship's wheel, which could spin freely or be locked in place with a clutch. Colt spent many hours aboard ship carving a wooden prototype revolver. After returning from sea, Colt spent a couple of years perfecting his design funded by running a touring show, entertaining people with nitrous oxide (laughing gas). By 1836 Colt had been granted both British and American patents for his designs and he began selling the revolvers, but business was at first slow. It was not until 1846, when the American government was expanding its territory into Texas and sought a new weapons supplier, that Colt got his break – he signed a contract with the American Army to supply 1,000 Colt revolvers. With this hefty contract Colt was able to streamline his business, creating an efficient production line in a manufacturing plant where he could produce 150 weapons a day. The success of the Colt brand was in part due to Samuel Colt himself, who was a wily marketer, ensuring his weapons were gifted to royalty and seen in the hands of sportsman, explorers and heads of state. Colt died in 1862 a very wealthy man. Ten years after his death the Colt .45 was released, the gun for which his name would go down in history. The Colt .45 was nicknamed 'the gun that won the West' because it was the standard service revolver for the American army between 1873 and 1892 when it was crucial to American expansion.

CYRILLIC *Slavic alphabet*

The Cyrillic alphabet was developed in the tenth century; it forms the basis of more than fifty languages, including Russian, Ukrainian, Bulgarian and Serbian. The alphabet is named after St Cyril, who along with St Methodius of the Eastern Orthodox Church travelled into Moravia as a missionary. Disciples of these early missionaries then took their message into the Bulgarian Empire and developed the Cyrillic alphabet, based on capital Greek letters, in order to translate and disseminate tracts of the Bible. Originally forty-three letters made up the Cyrillic alphabet, but modern languages have become somewhat streamlined and today Russian uses a more modest thirty-two letters.

DAHLIA *genus of brightly flowering plants with tuberous roots, native to Mexico*

Dahlias were first noted by Europeans when Spanish explorer Francisco Hernández encountered them in 1570 during his voyage to Mexico. The Aztecs found many uses for the plant – eating the tuberous roots, using the hollow stems as water pipes and crushing up the plant as medicine. In 1789 the director of the Botanical Garden in Mexico City sent some seeds to Antonio José Cavanilles at the Botanic Garden in Madrid, who managed to grow them into plants, naming the new genus *Dahlia* after the Swedish botanist Andreas Dahl (1751–1789). Dahl was a student of the famed taxonomist Carl Linnaeus, and later worked on curating the *herbarium parvum* made up of duplicates from Linnaeus's personal herbarium. When dahlias were first introduced in Europe they were intended as food, the tubers dished up as an alternative to the potato. However, once the fashion for exotic flowers came to the fore in the Victorian era all thoughts of eating dahlias were shelved and they were cultivated and hybridized for their fabulous showy blooms.

DERRICK *a hoist crane*

Originally the word 'derrick' was used to refer to a hangman, but then over time came to mean the gallows themselves, before coming into usage to refer to a hoist crane – used to lift cargo from ships onto the dock. This circuitous route started with a famed hangman at Tyburn, London. Thomas (some sources have Godfrey) Derrick was active *c.* 1600. Such was his infamy that he was frequently referred to in contemporary popular theatre and as a consequence his name became associated with the gallows themselves. Recruiting a hangman was not easy; few people were keen to take on such a gruesome role, and so novel methods were used to find the man for the job. Derrick was a convicted rapist; the Earl of Essex promised to pardon him if he would take on the role of hangman. Derrick readily agreed. It was something of a **HOBSON'S CHOICE** (see page 61), the other option being to accept the death penalty himself. Clearly a perfectionist, Derrick was not content to just sling a rope over the gallows; instead he invented a series of pulleys to make the whole process more efficient – and it was this innovation which ultimately led to his association with hoist cranes, which utilize a similar technique. In a strange quirk of fate, in 1601 Derrick executed the very man who had got him the job: Robert Devereux, Earl of Essex, who had staged an unsuccessful coup against the government.

DIESEL *a type of internal combustion engine; a type of fuel*

Rudolf Diesel (1858–1913) was a French–German engineer who invented the simple yet efficient diesel engine in 1893. At this time the motor car was in its early infancy and a cheap, reliable and streamlined engine was desperately needed. Diesel used his knowledge of thermodynamics to develop a compression-ignition engine which was far more efficient than any other engine on the market, but unfortunately it was, at least initially, unreliable. Diesel continued to refine his engine and began to see some success – by 1904 his engines were being used in French submarines. The fuel used in Diesel's engines, which was heavier and cheaper to produce, also became known as 'diesel'. Despite the growing success of his design, Diesel was beset by financial problems. While travelling aboard the steamer *Dresden*, on his way to a meeting in London, he fell into the sea to his death. Numerous conspiracy theories implicating oil companies or even the German government exist, but the most likely explanation appears to have been suicide. Diesel stepped out of his cabin during the evening of 29 September 1913 (a date which had been marked with a cross in his diary), leaving his nightshirt neatly folded on the bed, and never returned. His decomposed body was later found at sea. Diesel did not live to see the huge success of his invention, which after World War I grew massively in popularity, becoming the dominant engine type in trucks, ships and trains.

DOM PÉRIGNON *a prestigious vintage champagne*

Many myths have grown up around Dom Pérignon (1638–1715), a Benedictine monk and cellar master at Hautvillers Abbey in the Champagne region of France, which ultimately led to his name being adopted as the moniker of a celebrated vintage champagne. Pérignon's true role in the development of winemaking was vital, but his part in the invention of sparkling champagne is pure fantasy. From the thirteenth century the wine produced in the Champagne region of France was actually a light red, similar to Burgundy, and one of the many aims of Dom Pérignon was to banish the bubbles from his wine. The fastidious monk soon established a number of practices which revolutionized modern wine-making – such as only picking quality grapes, harvesting in the cool early morning and hard-pruning the vines to keep them below 3 feet in height, thus boosting their yield. These innovations meant that the wine produced at Hautvillers was of superior quality and soon many neighbouring vineyards were following Pérignon's lead and sharing his wisdom. Due to Dom Pérignon's influence on the local Champagne wines he became celebrated in the region, and in the 1820s an enterprising successor at Hautvillers, Dom Groussard, created the myth that Pérignon had invented sparkling wine, thereby immediately boosting the fortunes of the area. Effervescent champagne as we know it today was first developed in the 1700s; the first champagne house, Maison Ruinart, was established in 1729, starting a trend of exclusivity. In the 1920s the famed house of Moët et Chandon decided to produce a vintage champagne, and chose the name Dom Pérignon to associate itself with the legendary winemaker. The myths linking him to the invention of champagne only served to cement the popularity of the prestigious cuvée.

DOUGLAS FIR *a species of pine tree native to the Pacific Northwest of America*

David Douglas (1799–1834) was a Scottish botanist who in 1824 was chosen to take part in a plant-collecting expedition to the American Pacific Northwest. The expedition was a huge success and Douglas is credited with introducing at least 240 species of plants to Britain, including numerous conifers such as ponderosa pine, western white pine, sugar pine, Sitka spruce and, of course, the Douglas fir *(Pseudotsuga menziesii)*. While exploring in Oregon he collected the dried branches and needles of a tree he named 'Oregon pine', which he sent back to England. It was this tree which was later named Douglas fir in his honour, the Latin name recognizing the role of his colleague (and rival) Archibald Menzies in its discovery. The introduction of these trees to Britain had a great impact not only on the landscape but also on the timber trade. The Douglas fir became the most commercially important tree in North America. Douglas visited Hawaii in 1833 on a plant-collecting expedition and there suffered a mysterious death. The last person to see him alive was Ned (Edward) Gurney, a hunter and escaped convict, who reported that Douglas died after climbing the Mauna Loa volcano where he fell into a pit trap and was crushed by a bull which fell on top of him. Suspicion fell on Gurney due to his shady past and the rumour that Douglas had been carrying more money than was returned by Gurney with his body. The truth of his untimely death may never be known. Today the place of his death is marked with numerous Douglas firs, planted in his honour.

DOW JONES *short for the Dow Jones Industrial Index, a key stock market index*

Charles Dow (1851–1902) was an unlikely financial trail-blazer, having never finished school, but his ideas and insights were to change forever investors' relationships with the companies they invested in. Dow was born on a farm in Connecticut; at the age of 18 he secured a job on his local newspaper, impressing his bosses with his financial reporting. In 1882 he moved to New York to work for the Kiernan News Agency. Spotting a gap in the market, Dow established Dow Jones & Company with statistician Edward Jones and silent partner Charles Bergstresser. They released their first two-page daily newspaper, the *Customer's Afternoon Letter* (which in 1889 was renamed the *Wall Street Journal*), in 1884. Dow's innovation was to publish investor information on the top companies in a daily stock table and to include quarterly and annual information on company performance. This had never been done before; in fact most companies shied away from sharing their financials with anyone but Wall Street insiders. So this democratizing of information was a massive shift. Dow saw that stock indexes could be very useful as a means of taking the temperature of the New York Stock Exchange as a whole and so he created the first Dow Jones Index in 1883. He reassessed his index in 1896, creating the Dow Jones Industrial Index, which tracked the closing price of shares in the top twelve companies and divided them by twelve at the end of the day, giving an average – a neat way to chart performance of the market as a whole. Today the Dow Jones continues to be one of the most important stock market indexes in the world; it includes thirty top American companies in its index.

DRACONIAN *excessively harsh (especially in relation to laws)*

Named after a Greek lawmaker named Draco, who was the first recorded legislator in Athens, 'draconian' has come to encompass anything overly severe. Prior to Draco's involvement most laws in Greece were oral or based around the tradition of blood feud, but in 621 BCE Draco became the first lawmaker to codify written laws, which he displayed for all to see on wooden tablets. The laws created by Draco were extremely authoritarian, with the death penalty a consequence for even minor infringements. Such was the excessive harshness of the Draconian laws that all except the homicide law were later repealed and his name became synonymous with especially strict or severe rules.

DUNCE *someone who is slow at learning*

The word 'dunce' has come to have strong associations with the humiliation of slow learners due to the Victorian habit of forcing poor students to stand on a stool wearing a dunce's cap when they failed at their lessons. However, the word is conversely named after a noted intellectual, John Duns Scotus (1265–1308), whose legacy was slowly eroded by changing religious ideas. Scotus – named for his place of birth, the village of Duns in Scotland – was ordained as a Franciscan monk. He grew into a philosopher and theologian of great repute, writing complex theses on the Immaculate Conception and proof of the existence of God. A school of philosophy, Scotism, grew in his wake. Scotus's intensely analytical theories and strict adherence to the Catholic scriptures were what ultimately led to his name becoming associated with the modern word 'dunce'. During the Protestant Reformation, Catholic philosophies and teachings were widely criticized, and many adherents of Scotism began to be characterized as slavish followers who were too stupid to think for themselves. It was this association that meant that by 1527 anyone espousing his theories became known as 'Duns' and considered intellectually inferior. Over the years the spelling morphed into 'dunce' and the word was applied more generally to a dullard or blockhead, completing the strange transformation of a respected intellectual into the word for the class dimwit.

EARL GREY TEA *tea blend flavoured with bergamot oil*

The exact reasons for this blend of tea being named Earl Grey are disputed but it is agreed that the tea was named in honour of Charles Grey (1764–1845) who became 2nd Earl Grey in 1807 on the death of his father. Grey was prime minister from 1830 to 1834, his notable achievements being parliamentary reform and Catholic Emancipation. Numerous stories relate how the tea came to be associated with Grey. In one version a diplomat of Grey's whilst visiting China saved the life of a mandarin, who in gratitude gifted a special blend of tea, which the diplomat took back to England for his master. Another story suggests that a batch of Chinese tea and a batch of bergamot were shipped together and the two flavours mingled pleasingly, so that when some of the tea was presented to Grey the blend was celebrated and subsequently caught on. A further, and perhaps the most plausible, story relates that Grey had a custom blend of tea created by a Chinese mandarin friend to complement (or disguise) the strongly flavoured water at his Northumberland home, Howick Hall. It was said that Lady Grey served this blend at their Northumberland and London homes and their special brew became fashionable. Research recently conducted by the *Oxford English Dictionary* threw yet more confusion into the mix after their calls for early references to Earl Grey tea to be brought to their attention. This indicated that the first instances of tea flavoured with bergamot were recorded in 1824. However, far from being the luxury blend it is today, this tea flavouring was used by tricksters to pass off low-grade teas as better quality.

EVEREST *the tallest mountain in the world*

In 1802 the Great Trigonometrical Survey to map the entire Indian subcontinent was launched by the British. The ambitious project faced many hurdles, including inhospitable terrain, monsoon and malaria, and yet the surveyors were remarkably accurate. It was soon established that the Himalayas and not the Andes, as previously thought, were the highest mountain range in the world and one particular peak was identified as the highest of them all, Peak XV. The surveyors measured the peak in 1856 and announced it was 29,002 feet above sea level (the most recent GPS measurements confirm it as 29,029 ft, revealing quite how accurate they were). George Everest (1790–1866) excelled in mathematics at school and on graduation set off for India to work on the Great Trigonometrical Survey. Initially Everest worked under Colonel William Lambton but was later promoted to Surveyor General of India in 1830. With the immense survey finally complete Everest retired back to

England in 1843 and was succeeded as Surveyor General of India by Andrew Waugh. Waugh was in charge when Peak XV was discovered to be the tallest mountain in the world and it was decided an official British name was required for this mountain, which in Nepal was known as Sagarmāthā. In 1865 Waugh proposed the mountain be named in honour of his predecessor to celebrate his dedication to the mapping of India. The ever-humble George Everest protested but was overruled by the Royal Geographical Society and Peak XV officially became Mount Everest.

FAHRENHEIT *temperature scale*

Daniel Gabriel Fahrenheit (1686–1736) was a German-born Dutch maker of scientific instruments. He lived most of his life in Amsterdam but travelled widely, using his trips to consult with other scientists and to research new techniques in instrument making. At first, Fahrenheit used an alcohol-based thermometer, but he desired greater accuracy in temperature readings and invented the mercury thermometer in 1714. At this time no scale for measuring temperature had been agreed and so in 1724 he proposed a new scale, which ranged from o to 212°, with 32° representing the freezing point of water and 212° the boiling point – the first internationally accepted measure of temperature. Fahrenheit continued to research the measurement of temperature and discovered that atmospheric pressure, and therefore altitude, affected the boiling point of water. Fahrenheit's scale has been tweaked over the years as measurement has become more accurate, but it has remained the most widely used temperature scale in the United States.

FALLOPIAN TUBES   *the tubes through which eggs pass from the ovaries into the uterus*

Gabriello Fallopio (1523–1562) was an influential Italian surgeon and anatomist who held the prestigious post of professor of anatomy at the University of Padua. Alongside Andreas Vesalius and Eustachius, he is revered as one of the fathers of modern anatomy. Fallopio initially studied the anatomy of the head, but his observations on the reproductive system are what he is best remembered for after he became the first to describe the fallopian tubes. Fallopio was an extremely fastidious and detailed dissectionist, as confirmed by his book *Observationes anatomicae* (1561), and attested to by the many parts of the body he first gave names to, including the cochlea, placenta, clitoris, palate, and vagina. Fallopio was also a keen botanist, becoming superintendent of the botanical garden at Padua. He has also been remembered in the naming of the genus *Fallopia* – of which the notorious Japanese knotweed is a member.

FERRIS WHEEL   *rotating fairground ride in the shape of a wheel*

After the success of the 1889 World Fair held in Paris, with the Eiffel Tower as its centrepiece, the pressure was on Chicago to create a similarly spectacular landmark. Architects, inventors and visionaries queued up to make suggestions (Eiffel even suggested a taller version of his tower), but it was engineer George Washington Gale Ferris Jr (1859–1896) who came up with the winning design – an enormous rotating wheel. The original Ferris wheel, as it became known, was 250 feet wide, and had thirty-six cars which could hold forty people per car. When the wheel was unveiled in June 1893 at the World's Columbian Exposition it became an immediate sensation. During the nineteen weeks it was open, over 1.4 million people paid their 50 cents for a twenty-minute ride on the wheel and an unparalleled view of Chicago. Unfortunately after the closure of the fair the ride fell dormant, and in 1896, beset by debts and illness, Ferris died at just 37 years old. The wheel was later sold to the St Louis Exposition in 1904, but this was its last hurrah and in 1906 it was dynamited and scrapped. Despite the ignoble ending of the original Ferris wheel, the design was much copied and has become a staple at fairs and as an attraction in major cities across the world.

FOLEY ARTIST *sound-effects artist*

In the 1920s, as film-makers first experimented with the use of sound, one man, Jack Donovan Foley (1891–1967), created a whole new method to enhance the sound on the screen. Foley worked behind the scenes directing inserts for close-up shots in films. After the success of *The Jazz Singer* (1927) other major studios began adopting sound. Foley embraced this early technology and took to performing the sound effects, such as footsteps, rustling clothes, backfiring cars and clinking glasses, live in post-production to enhance the sounds. Foley was such a professional that he would imitate an actor's walk, perfecting the noise and pace of their feet hitting gravel, and ensuring that the sounds exactly synchronized with the pictures. Foley worked on numerous films over the years but was given no billing in the credits. However, his artistry was immortalized in the naming of this new profession 'foley artists' and in the numerous other eponyms relating to his trade: foley studio, foley editor, foley sheets.

FOXTROT *a ballroom dance*

The foxtrot is performed to big-band music and follows a slow–quick–quick step motion. It is said to have been invented by vaudeville performer Harry Fox in 1914 when he began performing a fast yet simple trotting dance along to a ragtime song during his performances at the New York Theatre. The dance was immediately popular with the public, who began imitating it at clubs, and by the end of 1914 the American Society of Professors of Dancing had begun trying to standardize the dance in order to teach it. Dance teacher Oscar Duryea was tasked with modifying the dance as the constant trotting was deemed too exhausting. As a result, Duryea introduced a gliding element. Hugely popular husband-and-wife team Vernon and Irene Castle soon adopted and perfected the foxtrot, performing it to great acclaim at their dance shows and sealing its enduring popularity with the public.

FUDGE *to obscure the truth or botch a job*

Etymologists have proposed that this word derives from the sixteenth-century word *fadge*, which meant to 'make fit'. However, an alternative story traces the naval use of the term back to a real-life character named Captain Fudge, who was active in the late seventeenth century. Isaac D'Israeli (father of Benjamin) wrote in *Curiosities of Literature* (1791) that the verb 'to fudge' comes from a certain Captain Fudge (also known as Lying Fudge), who was famed for being economical with the truth. As a consequence, when sailors thought someone was lying they would cry out 'you fudge it', leading to the popularization of the term.

FULL MONTY, THE *to have, give or do everything possible*

This is a fairly modern phrase which, according to the *Oxford English Dictionary*, first came into common usage in the 1970s. Even so, its exact root is unclear. One of the most commonly cited theories is that the saying derives from the men's clothes shop Burton, the first branch of which opened in Chesterfield in Derbyshire in 1904. Sir Montague Burton (1885–1952) owned the very successful chain of shops, which sold off-the-peg suits, and it is thought customers asked for the 'full Monty' if they wanted the complete three-piece suit of trousers, jacket and waistcoat. An alternate theory is traced to Second World War hero Field Marshall Montgomery (1887–1976), who was fondly known as Monty. This version says that Monty demanded a full English breakfast every morning, even when serving in the blistering heat of the North African desert. This led to the English breakfast becoming known among soldiers as the 'full Monty', from where it spread into a more general meaning and usage.

GALVANIZE *to excite or inspire to action (as if stimulated by electricity)*

The root of this eponym derives from galvanism, whereby electricity is produced by chemical action. This phenomenon was first noted by Luigi Galvani (1737–1798), who during his experiments on frogs in the 1780s noticed that when his steel scalpel accidentally touched the brass hook holding the frog's leg, the leg twitched. Further experiments followed and in 1791 Galvani published a paper on his research suggesting that the twitching frog's legs indicated the existence of 'animal electricity' – the life force of the frog's muscles. On hearing of Galvani's 'discovery', Alessandro Volta, physics professor at the University of Pavia, respectfully disputed the finding, suggesting instead that it was the two different types of metal which had caused the leg to twitch and that the leg was not producing electricity but reacting to it. Volta thus coined the word 'galvanism' to describe Galvani's research into bioelectrics. Galvani's work in part inspired Volta's later invention of the **VOLTAIC** pile battery. 'Galvanize' as a verb, meaning to stimulate into action, came into common usage in the nineteenth century.

GARGANTUAN *enormously large*

Gargantua is a giant with an enormous appetite for food and drink invented by the French writer François Rabelais (*c*.1494–1553). Rabelais was a Renaissance humanist, monk, scholar and writer who used his considerable intellect to write bawdy, satirical tales which lambasted the pervasive superstitions of the era. Rabelais wrote five books on the giant Gargantua and his son Pantagruel, published between 1532 and 1564. The tales are fantastical, crude and amusing in equal measure. They reveal something of humanist views on education, which at the time were at odds with traditional Roman Catholic teaching; because of this the

Collège de la Sorbonne labelled the books obscene. The word 'gargantuan', inspired by the amiable yet voracious giant, made its way into common usage in the sixteenth century to describe something enormous. It is likely that Rabelais created the word from the Spanish/Portuguese root *garganta*, which means throat or gullet.

GERRYMANDER *to make boundary changes to an electoral region in order to favour a particular party*

The practice of gerrymandering is as old as American politics but the word itself was coined on 26 March 1812 after the *Boston Gazette* printed a cartoon satirizing the bizarre shape of the new electoral district of Governor Eldridge Gerry. The Governor of Massachusetts had signed a bill to reshape the district in 1812 in order to favour his Democratic-Republican Party over the Federalists. A cartoonist at the Gazette, Elkanah Tisdale, noted the similarity with a lizard, adding a head, teeth and claws to a drawing of the map and naming it 'The Gerry-mander' in a portmanteau of the governor's name and a salamander lizard. Both the term and the cartoon proved very popular and were widely reproduced in newspapers across America in 1812, popularizing the term, and by 1848 it had been included in a dictionary, cementing the neologism for a political practice that was rife.

GREENGAGE *a variety of plum with green-gold skin and flesh*

The greengage plum originated in Armenia and from there was imported to France, where it was named *Reine Claude* (Queen Claude) in honour of Queen Claude, duchess of

Brittany (1499–1524). In 1724 Sir William Gage, 2nd Baronet of Hengrave (c.1650–1727), brought the plum to England, where it found great popularity and was named in his honour. One possibly apocryphal story recounted by Sir Joseph Banks in *Transactions of the Royal Horticultural Society* in 1812 is that when the fruit trees were transported to Britain the plant labels were all intact except for that of the *Reine Claude*. Thus when the tree fruited his gardener scrawled onto the label 'the Green Gage' and the name was coined.

GROG *alcohol*

Admiral Vernon (1684–1757) was a celebrated English naval commander who fought many battles against the Spanish. In 1739 he scored a great victory, taking the Spanish town of Porto Bello in Panama with only six ships – a victory which resulted in the naming of the famous street in London 'Portobello Road' and inspired the song 'Rule, Britannia'. Vernon was nicknamed 'Old Grog' as he often sported a grogram coat (a rough woollen garment), and so when in 1740 he ordered that sailors' ration of rum be watered down with water (three parts water to one part rum), to reduce drunkenness, the drink became known as 'grog'. Water kept aboard ship tended to become brackish and slimy with algae and the ration of rum was used to make the drinking water more palatable. Vernon also added lemon to his water stores; this addition to improve the taste had the added bonus of a dose of vitamin C, which helped keep scurvy at bay – an innovation that was soon adopted across the navy once the cause of scurvy was identified by James Lind in 1747. Grog was not the only thing named after

Admiral Vernon. Lawrence Washington, half-brother of George Washington, served under Admiral Vernon; when he inherited his father's estate, then named Little Hunting Creek, he decided to rename it **MOUNT VERNON** in his old boss's honour. When Lawrence himself died the estate passed to George Washington, who kept the name.

GUILLOTINE *execution machine consisting of a sharp blade which drops between a wooden frame to swiftly sever the head*

Not all eponyms bring joy to their namesake. Pity poor Dr Joseph-Ignace Guillotin (1738–1814), for he was opposed to capital punishment and yet his name has been adopted as the moniker for a machine which claimed thousands of lives. Prior to the French Revolution a number of crude execution machines had existed, such as the medieval Halifax Gibbet, but most capital punishment was carried out with a sword or axe and unfortunately was frequently botched. In 1789, Guillotin, a deputy of Paris, suggested to the French National Assembly that an execution machine which was fast and efficient would be more humane. Dr Antoine Louis, secretary of the Academy of Surgery, designed the prototype; the first Louisette (as it was initially known) was crafted by Tobias Schmidt, a German harpsichord maker. The first victim (a highwayman) was beheaded by the machine on 25 April 1792. It soon became popularly known as the guillotine, later becoming the weapon of choice against the enemies of the French Revolution, with thousands losing their lives to the device, including King Louis XVI and Marie Antoinette. Guillotin was horrified that his name had become associated with the guillotine and tried to distance himself from the machine, petitioning the government to change its name. When this failed, the family themselves changed their names to escape the gruesome association. The guillotine continued to be used as a method of execution in France right up until 1977. The death penalty was abolished in France in 1981.

GUPPY *colourful tropical fish*

Guppies are bright tropical fish native to the Caribbean and South America. They were first described by Wilhelm Peters in 1859 in Venezuela and he gave them the scientific name *Poecilia reticulata*. This name was superseded in 1866 after Robert John Lechmere Guppy (1836–1916), school inspector and amateur naturalist, caught a specimen off the coast of Trinidad and sent it to the British Museum in London. Taxonomist Albert Günther named the specimen *Girardinus guppii* in Guppy's honour and the common name 'guppy' caught on. Unfortunately scientists continued to argue over the correct Latin name for the species, and in 1913 it was reclassified as *Lebistes reticulatus* and again in 1963 back to its original name *Poecilia reticulata*. Throughout this nomenclative commotion the common name 'guppy' stuck, and the colourful little fish found its way into many aquariums across the world, becoming one of the most popular types of tropical pet fish.

HALLEY'S COMET *famed comet which returns to Earth every seventy-five years*

The first known report of Halley's Comet was in a Chinese chronicle which noted its journey through the sky in 239 BCE.

Historically comets were thought to be omens or heralds, and most famously William the Conqueror took Halley's Comet as a positive sign when he watched it blaze across the sky in 1066 before his invasion of England – the Bayeux Tapestry, which chronicles the invasion, includes the comet, indicating its significance. Astronomer Edmond Halley (1656–1742) was born in 1656 and went on to study at Oxford. Halley was inspired by Astronomer Royal John Flamsteed's work recording stars in the northern hemisphere to create his own catalogue of stars in the southern hemisphere, a work he completed by 1678, earning him plaudits and a fellowship of the Royal Society. In 1705 Halley published the work for which he became most famed: *A Synopsis of the Astronomy of Comets*. Halley had researched historical references to comets and realized that three descriptions from 1531, 1607 and 1682 were so similar in orbit that they probably represented the same comet returning to Earth – the first time anyone had suggested a comet might recur. Halley predicted that the comet would fly past Earth again in 1758, which it did, but unfortunately he did not live to see it as he died in 1742. However, the comet was now named in his honour in recognition of his role in identifying it and pushing forward human understanding of the way comets orbit. Halley's Comet last passed Earth in 1986 and is scheduled to reappear in 2061.

HECTOR *to intimidate or bully someone with words*

The character of Hector in Greek legend is most famously drawn in Homer's *Iliad*. Hector is portrayed as an ideal hero – a great son, warrior, husband, friend and father – proving his many attributes during the Trojan War. In battle Hector, a prince of Troy, killed Patroclus, a great friend of the Greek hero Achilles. As a consequence Achilles, in an act of revenge, pursued Hector, killed him and then in a public act of retribution dragged his dead body behind his chariot as he rode round the tomb of Patroclus. Despite the harsh treatment of Hector's corpse, the gods ensured that it remained uncorrupted, and when the body was finally returned to his father, King Priam, for burial Hector's body was intact. This legend means that initially the word 'Hector' was used to describe a valiant hero; however, by the seventeenth century the name had taken on the slang connotation of 'to bluster, bully or domineer'. It is possible this meaning, which remains to this day, grew from Hector's rallying speech in the *Iliad* in which he implores his fellow Trojans to keep fighting against the Greeks.

HEIMLICH MANOEUVRE *method to rescue choking victims by abruptly squeezing the victim's abdomen in an upwards movement to dislodge the blockage*

Dr Henry Heimlich (1920–2016) was an American thoracic surgeon who invented and popularized the anti-choking method the 'Heimlich manoeuvre' – a name coined by the *Journal of the American Medical Association* in his honour in 1974. Choking has always been a common cause of death, especially among children, and Heimlich was inspired to develop and promote a simple method to counteract it. He first proposed his treatment in an article entitled 'Pop Goes the Café Coronary' in *The Journal of Emergency Medicine* in 1974 but initially his ideas were criticized as too risky – the hard upward thrust above the victim's navel was deemed difficult for an ordinary person to carry out safely and correctly. However, Heimlich persisted and sent his idea to many national newspapers, which printed the instructions. Anecdotal evidence soon emerged from across America to suggest a number of people had followed the advice and saved lives. With a growing body of evidence that the manoeuvre worked, government bodies across the globe began to promote and approve the treatment and it soon spread into public consciousness. The Heimlich Institute has estimated that 50,000 lives in the United States have been saved by the Heimlich manoeuvre and no doubt countless more across the wider world.

HIPPOCRATIC OATH *an oath taken by doctors to uphold ethical standards of care*

Many doctors on graduating from medical school still recite the Hippocratic Oath (or at least a modern version) promising to practise medicine according to their best abilities and in the best interests of their patients. The Oath, one of the oldest ethical codes in the world, was formulated by one of the fathers of modern medicine, Hippocrates (*c.* 460–370 BCE). Although little is known about the life of Hippocrates, his medical ideas have been preserved as he left behind a twelve-volume work, known as the Hippocratic Collection, which contains medical writings from many Ancient Greek intellectuals, including himself. Hippocrates was one of the first doctors to argue for the separation of religion and medicine, stating that disease was caused by lifestyle or environmental factors, not punishment from the gods.

This distinction allowed medicine to be studied in its own right and precipitated medicine as a profession. It was not until the 1700s that the Hippocratic Oath was translated into English and became part of the graduation ceremony for doctors. In 1948 it was updated and incorporated into a new oath, dubbed the Declaration of Geneva, which was adopted by the World Medical Association, upholding the ancient tradition of ethical medical practice.

HOBSON'S CHOICE *take it or leave it*

Thomas Hobson (*c.*1544–1631) made his fortune as a carrier – delivering newspapers and mail from Cambridge to London – and as an innkeeper. Hobson remains in the public consciousness due to the term 'Hobson's choice' – a saying that came into popular use after the manner in which he rented out his horses. Hobson kept a busy stable and when his horses were not delivering the mail he would rent them out to students and scholars. Hobson soon noticed that the fastest and strongest horses were the most popular and thus they became exhausted, while the slower horses were rarely picked. To counteract this, he employed a strict rotation system, in which anyone trying to hire a horse would have to choose the next one in line – effectively offering a particular horse or no horse at all. This successful method of 'take it or leave it' soon made Hobson very wealthy and ensured that his name would live on in the saying that sums up his ethos. The poet John Milton (1608–1674), who studied at Cambridge 1625–29, was clearly very impressed with Hobson's entrepreneurial spirit. After Hobson's death, Milton wrote a number of poems in memory of him, including 'On the University Carrier' and 'Hobson's Epitaph', in which he popularized the notion of Hobson's choice, ensuring that this Cambridge expression became familiar across the country.

HOOVER *to vacuum; a vacuum cleaner*

Janitor and inventor James Murray Spangler (1848–1915) invented the first upright vacuum cleaner in 1908 in an attempt to improve his asthma with more efficient cleaning. Spangler manufactured the machine himself in Canton, Ohio, after gaining a patent, but struggled to market it to a wider public. William Henry Hoover (1849–1932), an American leather-goods manufacturer, came across the design and, seeing its potential, purchased the patent from Spangler. Hoover improved on the design and came up with a clever strategy to improve sales of the expensive machine – customers were offered a free ten-day trial. This proved highly effective and by 1922 the company, now known as Hoover, was the largest vacuum-cleaner manufacturer in the world. In 1919 Hoover opened a factory in England and their vacuum cleaners soon became very popular, dominating the market, to the extent that 'hoovering' became synonymous with vacuuming. Despite the growth of other vacuum brands the word 'hoover' has maintained its meaning in Britain and Ireland, much to the frustration of other manufacturers.

HUDSON RIVER *river in New York State, USA*

Italian explorer Giovanni da Verrazzano was the first European to record what is today known as the Hudson River, in 1524. However, he assumed it was simply an estuary and did not follow its course, so it remained largely ignored for over seventy years until British explorer Henry Hudson (*c.*1565–1611) arrived on the scene. Hudson had undertaken a number of Arctic voyages to search for the fabled Northwest Passage – a short route through the Arctic from Europe to Asia – but had been forced to turn back due to ice. In 1609 Hudson once again set sail up the Atlantic coast of America in search of the route. Acting on a tip from American settlers he sailed past the island of Manhattan, approximately 150 miles up the Hudson River, as far as modern-day Albany. Hudson soon surmised that the river did not in fact connect through to the Pacific and turned back. However, his exploration of the region opened up the area for Dutch colonization. In 1610 Hudson embarked on a further expedition, this time to Canada, where he discovered what would subsequently be called Hudson Bay. Once again, though, Hudson was disappointed not to discover a Northwest Passage and the expedition lost its focus, the ship aimlessly sailing along the Canadian coast with the crew begging to return home. Hudson had alienated much of his crew by playing favourites, and when he had the crew's belongings searched to supplement dwindling supplies they mutinied. In June 1611, Hudson, his young son and seven others were forcibly cast adrift in a small open boat on Hudson Bay; they were never seen again. Despite Hudson's ignoble end, he is remembered as an important explorer and his memory lives on in the river and bay which took his name.

HYGIENE *promoting and preserving cleanliness and good health*

The root of this word comes from Hygieia, the Greek goddess of good health. Hygieia was the daughter of Asclepius, the god of medicine, and Epione, the goddess of healing. She and her sisters represented different aspects of health and healing – Panacea was the goddess of universal remedy, Iaso represented recuperation, Aceso was the goddess of the healing process, and Hygeia was the personification of good health. In art Hygeia is frequently depicted feeding a serpent from a cup.

JACQUARD *an elaborately patterned woven material; a loom using perforated cards*

Joseph-Marie Jacquard (1752–1834) revolutionized the weaving industry when in the early 1800s he developed the Jacquard loom. Jacquard's innovation was to introduce a system in which a punched card represented the intricate pattern to be woven, allowing machines to be worked by unskilled workers to quickly produce sought-after patterned damask and brocade. Skilled weavers rebelled against the modernization of their trade and attacked both Jacquard and the looms themselves (much like the Luddites, see page 71), but such were the commercial advantages of the Jacquard loom that it soon caught on across France and from there Britain and the rest of the world. It is thought that Jacquard's leap to using punched cards to relay a series of instructions to a machine were an important step in the later development of computers; Charles Babbage is known to have been inspired by Jacquard's technique. The new improved Jacquard loom meant that luxury patterned fabrics could be woven with relative ease, and as a consequence this type of fabric became known as jacquard.

JACUZZI *luxurious bath with water jets to produce bubbles*

Candido Jacuzzi was born in 1903 in Italy and emigrated with his six older brothers and six sisters to America, where they settled in Berkeley, California. The family set up a small engineering business, manufacturing airplane propellers. During World War I the Jacuzzis developed a monoplane and invented a series of submersible pumps, which brought great success to the firm, allowing them to open factories across North and South America. In 1949 Candido's young son, Kenneth, was diagnosed with rheumatoid arthritis and was recommended a course of hydrotherapy. At this time the only hydrotherapy available was in large communal baths at hospitals and so Candido invented a portable pump which could be used in a bathtub at home. The Jacuzzis realized the potential of the product and soon the company developed it commercially, finding modest success. In 1968, the third-generation Roy Jacuzzi created a version which incorporated the pump into the tub itself, effectively inventing what would become the hugely successful whirlpool bath. This new idea of a luxury hot tub marketed as a leisure item took off in the 1970s and the name Jacuzzi became synonymous with the product.

JCB *generic name for a mechanical digger*

In October 1945 Joseph Cyril Bamford bought a second-hand welding set for £1, with which he made a tipping trailer using steel from old air-raid shelters in his rented lock-up garage in Uttoxeter, Staffordshire. Bamford sold his first trailer for £45 and immediately began making another. By 1948 he was employing six people in the business and had developed the first hydraulic tipping trailer in Europe. Bamford continued to expand the company and introduce new product lines. By 1950, in a feat of marketing genius, he was painting all the vehicles yellow, creating a memorable brand. The logo JCB (after Bamford's initials) was introduced in 1953. Soon the company was manufacturing numerous heavy-lifting and loading vehicles. Today JCB has eighteen factories around the world and employs over 12,000 people, producing a range of more than 300 products. Despite this diversity, due to the recognizable yellow branding, in Britain the abbreviation JCB has become a generic term for any backhoe loader or digger.

KALASHNIKOV *alternative name for the AK-47 assault rifle*

Mikhail T. Kalashnikov (1919–2013) was born to a family of peasants in Siberia. He was conscripted into the Red Army in 1938. He was fascinated by weaponry and while working as a tank commander he began designing weapons. Superiors soon noticed his talents and he was assigned to work on designing a new rifle for the Soviet military. In 1947 Kalashnikov and his team came up with the AK-47 assault rifle (AK comes from *Avtomat Kalashnikova*, representing the designer and the rifle's automatic firing capability, and 47 from the year the rifle was first tested). The AK-47 was not especially innovative; however, it combined technology from a number of existing weapons to create a powerful, easy-to-use and cheap-to-manufacture rifle. The AK-47 was soon adopted by the Soviet army, which then shared the design with their allies, leading to huge numbers being manufactured and distributed across Eastern Europe and beyond. In recent years historians have voiced doubts over whether Kalashnikov was solely responsible for designing the iconic weapon. Nevertheless his rise from peasant to weapons designer fitted neatly into the Soviet propaganda machine and the role of his colleagues faded into the background. Ultimately the Kalashnikov has become one of the most famous weapons in the world, beloved by terrorists, mercenaries, criminals and soldiers alike.

KILNER JAR *sealed sterile jar for preserving fruit*

John Kilner established his glass bottle company in Yorkshire in 1842, producing glass jars and bottles for preserving fruit, vegetables, jams and preserves. Kilner died in 1857 and the firm passed on to his four sons and became known as Kilner Brothers. Towards the end of the nineteenth century the Kilners received a patent for their famous pressure-sealed system in which a rubber-sealed lid is screwed on to a glass jar, which is then submerged in a bath of boiling water to produce a vacuum seal, ensuring no bacteria can remain in the jar and thus keeping the contents from spoiling. The company in this period enjoyed great success, winning medals for its products at international trade fairs; by 1894 it employed 400 people and produced 300,000 glass bottles and jars a week. Unfortunately commercial pressures and competition saw the company flounder and in 1937 it filed for bankruptcy, selling off its patents for Kilner and Mason jars to American firm United Glass Bottle Company. Kilner jars have maintained their popularity, retaining their eponymous name; since 2000 the brand has been owned and the jars produced by the British Rayware Group.

KUIPER BELT *a disc-shaped region of the universe beyond Neptune, full of icy objects*

When Dutch astronomer Gerard Kuiper (1905–1973) first proposed the existence of the region now known as the Kuiper Belt in 1951 it was just a theoretical suggestion. Building on the work of Kenneth Edgeworth, who in 1943 had suggested that comets might exist beyond Neptune, Kuiper used the fact that, despite their finite existence, new comets continued to enter the solar system to extrapolate that there must be a source of objects beyond Neptune. In recognition of Edgeworth's contribution to the theory, some scientists now call it the Edgeworth–Kuiper Belt, but it is most widely known as the Kuiper Belt. The existence of the Belt was not confirmed until 1992, when astronomers David Jewitt and Jane Luu identified the first Kuiper Belt Object (KBO) known as 1992QB1. Since then our understanding of this region teeming with icy objects has increased, and further KBOs and various dwarf planets, such as Ceres, have been identified. It has been estimated that the Kuiper Belt is host to over a trillion comets.

LABRADOR *a peninsula in Canada; a breed of retriever dog*

Little is known about the Portuguese explorer João Fernandes Lavrador (1453–*c.*1501), after whom the peninsula is probably named, but it is thought he was originally from the Azores. Lavrador, who was known by his original profession or rank in life (*lavrador* means farmer or labourer in Portuguese), was issued a royal patent in 1499. He had connections to John Cabot (discoverer of Newfoundland, see page 8) and the port of Bristol, and it is thought he sailed as far as Greenland, naming it Terra do Lavrador. Early map-makers adopted this name but migrated it south to the Labrador Peninsula in eastern Canada. The first settlers in Labrador and Newfoundland were mostly fisherman who were resident for just the summer months when the fish were most prolific. These early settlers bought water dogs with them known as St John's dogs. These dogs, with a short-haired water-repelling coat, spent all day retrieving fishing lines and stray fish from the icy waters, proving invaluable to the burgeoning community. The longer-haired variety was selectively bred to create the larger, fluffier Newfoundland dog, and the smaller short-haired St John's dog was exported to England, where it was much in demand as a hunting dog. The line of Labrador retrievers which are so popular today began with keen hunter James Harris, the 2nd Earl of Malmesbury, who imported St John's dogs from Canada in the early 1800s and began breeding them. Just a few years later Walter Scott, the 5th Duke of Buccleuch, also began breeding the dogs. In the 1880s these two aristocratic families exchanged dogs to expand their breeding programmes and ensure the survival of this popular new breed, which was recognized by the Kennel Club in 1903. Thus the dogs originated in Newfoundland but were mistakenly named after the nearby Labrador Peninsula, which was itself named after a man who never set foot on its shores.

LEOTARD *close-fitting garment worn by gymnasts and dancers*

Jules Léotard (*c.* 1842–1870) was a French circus performer. As a child he had proven very adept at gymnastics, excelling on the parallel bars; this led him to invent the flying trapeze act. Léotard would practise his act for hours at home, his trapeze suspended over his father's swimming pool to prevent any hard landings. He debuted his flying trapeze at the Cirque Napoléon in 1859, where he somersaulted above the guests as they ate their dinner. Such was the success of his act that Léotard was engaged as the chief aerialist at the Cirque Franconi in Paris, and later performed in Britain, taking the stage at the Alhambra in London in 1861. The crowds flocked to see Léotard, and women were soon swooning over his graceful all-in-one knitted outfit, which showed off his hunky physique. Léotard continued to perform across Europe in circuses, pleasure gardens and music halls – on occasion stunning the crowd by leaping between five trapezes, performing a somersault between each one. Unfortunately when Léotard was just 28 years old he caught an infectious disease, thought to be smallpox, whilst in Spain and died. Léotard's legacy became not just the flying trapeze act he made popular but also the practical, aerodynamic suit he wore to perform it. Léotard's fame ensured that his costume began to be referred to by his name: at first it was just worn by circus performers, but by the 1920s gymnasts and ballet dancers had also adopted the leotard.

LISTERINE *antiseptic mouthwash*

Joseph Lister (1827–1912) is known as the 'father of antiseptic surgery' after his pioneering work on reducing infection. Lister had a successful career as a surgeon before moving to Glasgow University in 1860 to become professor of surgery.

Inspired by Louis Pasteur's work on micro-organisms and germ theory (see page 90), Lister began to experiment with the use of chemicals during and after surgery. Lister's research indicated that using a dressing soaked in carbolic acid post-surgery caused infection levels to drastically drop, and he began to explore the impact of other measures such as hand-washing, sterilizing surgical instruments and spraying carbolic acid into the air as surgery was carried out. American doctor Joseph Lawrence was intrigued by Lister's work and decided to develop a surgical antiseptic, which he named Listerine in honour of Lister. Lawrence sold his formula to a St Louis pharmacist, Jordan Wheat Lambert, in 1881 and Listerine was at first marketed as a surgical antiseptic, floor cleaner and cure for dandruff, but it saw little success. By 1914 Listerine was the first prescription product to be sold over the counter as a mouthwash. When in the 1920s Lambert's son, Gerald Barnes Lambert, started marketing Listerine as a cure for halitosis – bad breath rebranded as a medical condition – sales began to grow. The new market for antiseptic mouthwashes and bad-breath treatments exploded, with Listerine as the brand leader.

LUDDITE *one averse to new technology*

The Industrial Revolution in Britain of the late eighteenth and early nineteenth centuries brought immense changes to the labour force. As machines became more prevalent, traditional jobs were lost and many skilled workers felt undervalued. A movement sprang up, known as the Luddites, which protested against bad working conditions, arguing that skilled workers were being sidelined by factory owners using machinery to shortcut and flout traditional labour practices. The Luddites assembled in mass gatherings and destroyed factory machinery to make their point. The government reacted harshly, making the destruction of machines a capital offence, and sending soldiers to confront the rioters. By 1811 rumours had gone round that the leader of the Luddites was a shady character named Ned Ludd, also known as Captain, General or King Ludd. Soldiers searched far and wide for Ned Ludd, but they would never find him, for he was a mythical leader created to distract from the true organizers. Historians believe that the invented character of Ned Ludd was based on a real man who had inspired the movement some twenty-two years earlier. The real Ned Ludd, or Ludlam, was an apprentice at a textile factory in Leicester; when his boss criticized his sloppy weaving, the furious Ludd smashed up the machine in a fit of pique. It is thought this story entered local folklore and was used to inspire the growing movement, hence adopting Ludd's name and destructive methods. Ultimately, due to the draconian (see page 45) penalties handed out to the Luddites the movement was suppressed, but their spirit is kept alive in the continued use of the word to describe those averse to technology.

LYNCH *to kill someone, usually by hanging, without trial*

Lynching is an American term deriving from Lynch Law – meaning to give punishment without trial – its origins found in the American Revolutionary War of the 1780s. However, a certain amount of confusion remains over whom the term is named after because there were two prominent Lynches who claimed the eponym. The first, and most likely, is Colonel

Charles Lynch (1736–1796) of Bedford County, Virginia, who was an American Revolutionary plantation- and slave-owner. From 1778 he was a militia colonel and fervently sought out those with British loyalties and put them on informal trial. At this stage the punishments ranged from flogging to seizure of property. In a letter of 1782, Charles Lynch referred to the process as 'Lynch's Law', thought to be the first recorded use of the term. It seems likely that it was the actions of this prominent militiaman which popularized the term 'lynching' for mob execution without due trial. However, in 1836 Edgar Allan Poe claimed to have found a contract drawn up in 1780 between Captain William Lynch (1742–1820) of Pittsylvania County and his neighbours which used the term 'Lynch's Law' to describe their agreement to set up their own law without legal authority. Doubts have been cast over the veracity of this claim, partly because Edgar Allen Poe was well known as a literary hoaxer and also because Pittsylvania County and Captain William Lynch were obscure and as a result seem an unlikely source of a word which gained nationwide usage. Ultimately Lynch Law and the abominable practice of lynching gained traction during the American Civil War (1861–65), especially in the Deep South, where mobs of (usually white) people attacked and hanged (usually black) people without trial.

MACADAMIA *tasty nut in a hard woody shell*

The macadamia nut is native to Queensland in Australia. It has long been well known to the indigenous population, with many names among the various aboriginal tribes, including *jindilli* and *boombera*, and has been used for making flour, as a snack and as medicine. When Europeans arrived in Australia, an explorer named Allan Cunningham first described the tasty nut in 1828; however, he neglected to give it a scientific name, so among the settlers it became known as the Queensland nut or bush nut. In the 1850s botanists Walter Hill and Ferdinand von Mueller, director of the Royal Botanic Gardens in Melbourne, became the first to officially describe the trees that bear the nut after they came across it in the Queensland rainforest. They noted and classified two varieties of the tree, one with a smooth-shelled nut (*Macadamia integrifolia*) and the other with a rough-shelled nut (*Macadamia tetraphylla*), the genus named *Macadamia* after their friend and patron John Macadam. Macadam (1827–1865) was born in Glasgow and studied as a chemist. In 1855, aged 28, he set sail to Australia where he worked as an academic, teaching medicine and chemistry; advised the government on public health; and became a member of the legislative assembly of the self-governing colony of Victoria, earning the deep respect of his peers. Australians were slow to capitalize on the potential of the macadamia nut. In the 1890s macadamia trees were planted in Hawaii to act as windbreaks for the sugarcane fields. The nut became extremely popular and soon Hawaii was growing and exporting it to North America, leading many to assume the macadamia was native to Hawaii.

MACHIAVELLIAN *duplicitous, cunning and scheming behaviour for gaining power, usually in politics*

As a result of his writings on the subject Niccolò di Bernardo dei Machiavelli (1469–1527) is considered the father of political science – the study of the reality of political behaviour (rather than an idealized version). Machiavelli was a diplomat in Florence and worked during an era of intrigue and discord, as the ruling Medici family fell and then rose again to power. As a supporter of an independent Florence, Machiavelli was imprisoned and tortured when the city state was returned to papal control and the Medici regained power in 1512. After his release, rather than engaging again in public life, he focused instead on writing. Despite authoring numerous histories and treatises on politics, Machiavelli is best known, and demonized, for his short work *The Prince* (written in 1513 but not published until 1532), which reflects on political statecraft, portraying the unscrupulous motives and morals of those who scheme for power – the central theme being that the end justifies the means. It is this characterization that has linked Machiavelli's name with morally dubious politicians. When *The Prince* was published in 1532, after Machiavelli's death, it was immediately censored by Pope Clement VIII. It was not translated into English until 1640. It has remained a controversial book for its unflinching depiction of underhand political tactics, reminding us that in statecraft it is not always the virtuous who rise to the top.

MACKINTOSH *a long waterproof coat*

The waterproof mackintosh coat was named after the man who invented the fabric, Charles Macintosh (1766–1843). Macintosh worked as a chemist in Glasgow experimenting with naphtha, a by-product of coal tar, which he discovered could dissolve natural rubber to create a paste which could be sandwiched with material to make a waterproof fabric.

Macintosh received a patent for his fabric in 1823; in 1834 he founded his own company to manufacture waterproof coats because many local tailors refused to work with his product. In 1840 Macintosh moved the company to Manchester to merge with Thomas Hancock. The many uses for the waterproof material became apparent and soon production of rubberized coats boomed. Initially the coats were smelly and some melted in hot weather, but in 1843 Macintosh developed the use of vulcanized rubber, which improved the finish. Long waterproof coats became known as mackintoshes, inexplicably with an added *k*, probably due to the numerous spellings of the famous Scottish surname.

MAGNOLIA *evergreen tree or shrub with large cream/pink flowers*

The magnolia is an extremely ancient genus of tree, pollinated by beetles. The fossil record reveals that magnolias flourished across Europe 100 million years ago but were wiped out by the Ice Age. Today they are native only to Japan, China, North and South America. Both the ancient Chinese and the Aztecs used magnolias for medicinal and ceremonial purposes but the species was not described by a European until the seventeenth century. In 1688 a missionary in Virginia, John Bannister, sent a sample of *Magnolia virginiana* to Britain, thought to be the first magnolia plant in Europe for millions of years. In 1703 French botanist Charles Plumier (1646–1704) classified a tree he observed in Martinique as the genus *Magnolia* (today known as *Magnolia dodecapetala*) after fellow French botanist Pierre Magnol (1638–1715). Magnol was a very well-respected botanist; in 1689 he was the first to suggest grouping plants into seventy-six families – an innovation which aided the budding science of plant classification. The genus *Magnolia* was formally named after Magnol in 1737 by the father of plant taxonomy Carl Linnaeus.

MASOCHISM *gratification (sexual or otherwise) gained from one's own humiliation or pain*

When German psychiatrist Richard von Krafft-Ebing was compiling his pioneering work on human sexuality *Psychopathia Sexualis* (1886) he coined a number of new words, including 'homosexual', 'sadist' (see page 103) and 'masochist'. Krafft-Ebing chose the term 'masochism' after the Austrian novelist Leopold von Sacher-Masoch (1836–1895). Von Sacher-Masoch engaged in a masochistic relationship himself, with the fantastically named Fanny Pistor, with whom he signed a contract which allowed her to punish him for any minor transgression. He later used this relationship in his novella *Venus in Furs* (1870), in which the main character, Severin, also signs such a contract, becoming the slave of a woman who humiliates and ultimately leaves him for another man. When von Krafft-Ebing coined the word 'masochism', von Sacher-Masoch was still alive. Although he was unhappy to be associated with the term, by this time his health was waning so he had little energy to defend his reputation, and by 1895 he was dead. During his early career von Sacher-Masoch had been a celebrated writer but by the end he was becoming a laughing stock. The last nail in the coffin for his reputation came in 1906 when his ex-wife published her autobiography *My Confession*, in which she gave lurid details of his peccadilloes, such as his desire to have her whip him while dressed in furs, which caused a public scandal. Here, then, is an eponym which has proved more of a curse to a reputation than a blessing.

MAURITIUS *island in the Indian Ocean*

The first recorded visitors to the uninhabited island now known as Mauritius were Arabs in *c.*975, but they did not linger, and it was not until 1507 that it was visited again, this time by Portuguese sailors. In 1598 Dutch admiral Wybrand van Warwyck and his crew landed on the island, and gave it the name Mauritius, after Prince Maurice van Nassau, stadtholder of the Dutch Republic (1567–1625). In 1638 they established a small colony to exploit the ebony trees found on the island. By 1710 the Dutch had abandoned Mauritius and in 1715 the French took over, renaming it Isle de France, and establishing a sugarcane industry with the introduced species. During the Napoleonic Wars the island became strategically important and was invaded successfully by the British in 1810. They allowed the settlers to retain the French language and laws but restored the island's name to Mauritius. Independence from Britain was granted in 1968.

MAUSOLEUM *a magnificent stately tomb*

The original mausoleum was built in Halicarnassus (then a Greek city, today Bodrum in Turkey) in 353 BCE as the spectacular marble tomb for Mausolus, Persian satrap (governor) and king of Caria. Mausolus successfully ruled over the kingdom of Caria (in south-west Anatolia) for twenty-four years, expanding his territory and building many new cities, in the Greek style, along the coast of Asia Minor. The tomb was planned by Mausolus himself before his death, following which his wife Artemisia (who also happened to be his sister) oversaw the construction. The enormous monumental tomb was designed by Greek architects, Pythius and Satyros. It included statues of Mausolus and his queen, intricate bas-reliefs, and was topped with a marble chariot pulled by four horses. The mausoleum was so remarkable it was named one of the Seven Wonders of the Ancient World, but was sadly destroyed by an earthquake in the medieval period – the last of the six destroyed Wonders to become ruin. Due to the fame of Mausolas' stately tomb the word 'mausoleum' came into common usage to denote an especially magnificent burial place – a true monument to this ancient king.

MAVERICK *someone who does things their own way*

Samuel Augustus Maverick (1803–1870) was a lawyer and prominent landowner in Texas, holding over 385,000 acres. When 400 cattle came into his hands as part of a settlement, Maverick decided to keep them on his land. However, Maverick had no ranching experience and instead of branding all his cattle with his name, as was the norm, he left the cattle unnamed and allowed them to wander across his vast estate. Needless to say, when one of his cattle strayed into another rancher's territory they delighted in gaining a new addition to their herd and swiftly branded the unmarked cattle with their own name. Thus any unmarked cow became known as a 'Maverick'. The word entered into common usage to indicate someone who does things differently from the norm.

McCOY (THE REAL) *the genuine article*

As with many phrases, this word took a circuitous route from the original to the resulting eponym. It is thought the original phrase was in fact 'the real Mackay', originating with Scottish whisky distiller G. Mackay & Co. The first recorded use of the phrase was from an 1856 Scottish poem *Deil's Hallowe'en* which included the line 'a drappie [drop] o' the real McKay', which despite the different spelling most likely referred to the whisky brand and probably popularized the term in the UK and North America, to where the whisky was exported – this spelling was used in a letter by Robert Louis Stevenson in 1883. The change in spelling has many contenders vying for the eponym. One of the most likely is Scottish-Canadian inventor Elijah McCoy, who invented a machine to lubricate railway engines patented in 1872. It is thought that all copycat machines were inferior to McCoy's original and thus his product made use of the existing phrase to reassure customers. The other likely contender is an American champion boxer named Norman Selby (1872–1940), who was known as 'Kid McCoy'. Selby became welterweight champion in 1896, gaining fame across America and spawning many imitators. It is thought that Selby began to market himself as 'the real McCoy' to discredit any impostor. Somewhat ironically due to the popularity of the name McCoy, it is unlikely we will ever truly know who the original 'real McCoy' was.

MELBA TOAST *thin slivers of toast*

Dame Nellie Melba (1861–1931) was a world-famous opera singer born Helen Porter Mitchell in Victoria, Australia, and adopted the name Melba as a play on her beloved home city of

Melbourne. Melba rose to fame as a soprano; her outstanding voice enabled her to travel the world, gracing all the most celebrated stages – the Metropolitan in New York, La Scala in Milan, Covent Garden in London. Melba loved food and constantly fought to control her weight; fortunately she was a friend of the esteemed chef Auguste Escoffier, when he worked at the Savoy in London. It is thought he developed Melba toast in 1897 in Nellie's honour when she requested something plain after a bout of illness, and was delighted with the resultant crisp toasts, which then became a mainstay of the menu. Escoffier also developed **PEACH MELBA** – poached peach with raspberry sauce and ice cream – supposedly after Nellie told the chef she was worried that too much ice cream would harm her vocal chords; so he made her a special dish in which the ice cream was just a small element.

MENTOR *a wise counsellor*

Mentor is first mentioned as a character in Homer's *Odyssey*, which was composed in the eighth century BCE. Mentor was a friend of Odysseus and vowed to look after his home while he went to fight in the Trojan War. Later in the story the goddess Athena appears as Mentor to impart advice and guidance to Odysseus's son Telemachus when he is searching for his father. In 1699 François Fénelon wrote the romance *Les Aventures de Télémaque*, which made Mentor a central and important character, offering wise counsel. Fénelon's book was very popular and was translated into both English and German. Etymologists believe it is from his rendering of the character of Mentor that the term has come into usage in modern French and English to mean adviser.

MESMERIZE *to completely hold someone's attention so they can concentrate on nothing else*

Franz Anton Mesmer (1734–1815) was a German physician who came up with the theory of 'animal magnetism', which proposed that all animals had an invisible fluid within their bodies affected by the laws of magnetism. Mesmer believed that illness was caused by blockages in the flow of fluid around the body and that magnets could be used to unblock this fluid. In 1778 Mesmer moved to Paris where he caused quite a stir with his flamboyant healing technique, whereby he would 'cure' people of their blockages by stroking them with magnets and lulling them into a trance-like state, in what was to become a precursor to modern hypnotism. Unfortunately for Mesmer the medical establishment was very wary of his techniques and in 1784 a commission of scientists and doctors (including Benjamin Franklin and French chemist Antoine-Laurent Lavoisier) was set up to investigate his claims. The commission went on to report that there was no scientific basis for his theory of animal magnetism, and his mesmerist movement somewhat lost its momentum. Despite the disappointing end to his career, Mesmer's legacy now exists in his name, which has lived on to describe a feeling of captivation, and he has retrospectively been recognized for his contribution to the development of hypnosis.

MNEMONIC *a device to aid the memory*

Mnemonics have been used over the years to help school children remember key pieces of information. One of the most widely used is probably the mnemonic to remember the colours of the rainbow: Richard Of York Gave Battle In Vain (for red, orange, yellow, green, blue, indigo, violet). The word shares the same etymological root as Mnemosyne, the Greek goddess of memory – both deriving from the Greek word *mneme*, meaning epitaph, record or memory. Mnemosyne was one of the daughters of Uranus (god of the sky) and Gaia (goddess of the earth). Zeus slept with Mnemosyne for nine consecutive nights, resulting in the birth of the nine muses – Calliope (epic poetry), Clio (history), Euterpe (lyric poetry), Thalia (comedy and pastoral poetry), Melpomene (tragedy), Terpsichore (dance), Erato (love poetry), Polyhymnia (sacred poetry) and Urania (astronomy) – providing writers and artists with inspiration.

MOLOTOV COCKTAIL *improvised explosive device made from a bottle filled with flammable liquid, such as petrol*

This makeshift weapon, now synonymous with public resistance, was first put to use during the Spanish Civil War in the 1930s, but it was the outbreak of the Second World War that gave it its name. In 1939 the Molotov–Ribbentrop Pact was signed, effectively a Nazi–Soviet non-aggression pact, which saw the Nazis and Soviets carve up Europe into 'spheres of influence'. Thus, as the Nazis invaded Poland, the Soviets saw their chance to attack Finland. The Russians began to drop bombs on Helsinki, the Soviet foreign minister Vyacheslav Molotov wryly claiming that it was not bombs they were dropping but food parcels for the starving children. The bombs were thus nicknamed 'Molotov's bread baskets'. The Finns had had little time to prepare a defence force and so hundreds took to the streets using a crude home-made weapon – bottles filled with petrol, tar or other flammable liquid, with a rag in the top as a fuse. When lighted and thrown against a tank, the glass would shatter and the flammable liquid spread the fire into the tank's interior, forcing the soldiers to leave the confines of their vehicle, making them vulnerable to snipers. The Finns jokily nicknamed their weapon 'Molotov cocktails' as the drink to go with 'Molotov's bread baskets'. Although the Finns ultimately had to sue for peace by 1940, their resistance had ensured it was a Pyrrhic victory (see page 99) for the Russians, who had lost 300,000 men in the conflict. The Molotov cocktail's success as an improvised weapon saw its use spread throughout the Second World War, with Britain's home guard arming themselves in this way against a potential Nazi invasion. Post-war the Molotov cocktail remains the weapon of choice for rioters and protestors, retaining its place as a means of civil defence.

MORSE CODE *a method to electronically transmit messages using a series of long and short pulses*

Samuel Morse (1791–1872) was an American painter and inventor whose work on electricity led him to develop an electric telegraph machine. Throughout the 1830s and 1840s, Morse and colleagues Joseph Henry and Alfred Vail worked on developing the first telegraph, which was finally complete in 1844, when Morse was granted a patent. In order to send messages electronically, Morse needed to develop a method to quickly transmit sounds. He came up with the idea of using electronic beeps to represent dots and dashes, which could be codified to correspond to individual letters. Short signals, known as dits, were written as dots (and corresponded to one unit of time); long signals, known as dahs, were written as dashes. A pause of three units of time represented a pause between letters; a pause of seven units of time represented a gap between words. An operator could tap out the messages, which were sent over the telegraph, and printed out onto sheets of paper at the other end, which would then be translated back into English. Morse demonstrated his invention to Congress in 1844, sending what would be the famous message 'What hath God wrought' from Washington to Baltimore, thereby forever changing the speed at which we can communicate. Telegraphy quickly grew in popularity and by 1866 a cable had been laid beneath the Atlantic, allowing messages to be sent quickly from America to Europe. As Morse's code became more widely used, it no longer needed to be printed onto sheets; instead skilled operators could listen to the flurry of dits and dahs and translate them directly onto a telegram. Morse Code was adopted universally in 1865.

MUNROS *mountains in Scotland which stand at over 3,000 feet*

The Munros were first collated as a list of mountains over 3,000 feet by Sir Hugh Munro (1856–1919) in 1891 when he published them as 'Munro Tables' in the journal of the Scottish Mountaineering Club (SMC). Munro divided the summits into 283 separate mountains and also listed 255 other summits over 3,000 feet which he considered subsidiary and named 'Tops'. Munro's table caused much debate, as prior to his assertion it was believed that only about thirty mountains in Scotland topped 3,000 feet. Munro caught the mountaineering bug at the age of 17 when he went to study in Stuttgart and discovered the beauty of the Alps. When he returned to Scotland he established the SMC and became its first president. Munro did not manage to climb all the Munros in his lifetime. The first person to achieve this feat was the Rev. A.E. Robertson in 1901, starting a long tradition of 'Munro-bagging' among mountaineers. The list of Munros are overseen by the SMC and occasionally revised – most recently in 2012 when there were listed 282 Munros and 227 Tops.

NARCISSISM *the condition of being obsessed with one's own self/appearance*

In Greek mythology, Narcissus was an exceptionally good-looking young hunter. Everywhere he went women and men fell in love with him, but he showed them nothing but disdain. One day as he was hunting in the woods, the nymph Echo caught sight of Narcissus and instantly fell in love with him. Echo appeared to Narcissus and attempted to embrace him, but he recoiled and rode away. Devastated, Echo spent the rest of her days wandering disconsolately through the forest, no longer eating or drinking, until she faded away to nothing but her voice – becoming the ECHO of herself. In punishment for his cruel treatment of Echo, the god of retribution, Nemesis, caused Narcissus to catch sight of his reflection in a pool of water. Of course it was love at first sight and Narcissus could not tear his eyes away from the image of this beautiful youth. When Narcissus realized that he was in love with his own reflection, and not a flesh-and-blood person, he committed suicide in despair. His immortality was assured, however, not only by the eponym which represents self-love, but also in the flower narcissus, which is said to have sprung up from his spilled blood.

NEANDERTHAL *a now extinct human species which flourished during the last Ice Age*

The type specimen for this extinct human species was discovered in 1856 in Neanderthal (now known as Neandertal) in western Germany, and was named in 1864 by William King, who was the first to note that the skull belonged to a separate species. This, then, represents an eponym at one remove – because, although the species was named after a place, the place itself was named after a person, German hymn writer Joachim Neander (1650–1680). Born Joachim Neumann, he followed the fashion of the time and adopted the classical Greek version of his name: thus Neumann (which translates as 'new man') became Neander (from neo-ander). As a young man, Neander was rather boisterous but the course of his life changed in 1670 when he was inspired by the words of Pastor Theodore Under-Eyck. With his spiritual life awakened, Neander began to compose hymns, many of which rejoiced in the natural world, becoming the first major hymn writer for the German Reformed Church. In *c*.1850 the beautiful valley near Düsseldorf which had inspired Neander's hymns was renamed Neanderthal in his honour. In a strange twist, in 1901 the official spelling of the area was adapted to Neandertal; however, due to the laws of taxonomy the species first found there must retain the original spelling of Neanderthal.

NICOTINE *the active ingredient in the leaf of the tobacco plant*

Jean Nicot (1530–1600) was a French diplomat and scholar, who in 1557 was sent to Lisbon, Portugal, to negotiate a marriage between Margaret of Valois and the king of Portugal. While he was in Lisbon he met with the noted humanist Damião de Góis, who introduced him to the wonders of the tobacco plant. Nicot was instantly impressed and became convinced that tobacco could cure any number of ills, and in 1560 he sent samples of the seeds back to Catherine de' Medici in France. Nicot instructed the queen how to crush the tobacco leaves into a powder, which could then be sniffed through the nose to counteract various ailments. The habit soon became popular at court before spreading across France. Nicot then retired from court life and spent the rest of his days compiling a French dictionary, but it was not for this that he was to be remembered. The Swedish naturalist Carl Linnaeus in 1753 immortalized Nicot for his role in bringing tobacco to popularity by naming a genus of tobacco cultivars *Nicotiana*. Later, in 1828 when the active ingredient in tobacco was first identified it was given the name nicotine in his honour.

NOSY PARKER *someone who likes to pry into the affairs of others*

The traditional view is that the term 'nosy parker' derives from the Archbishop of Canterbury under Elizabeth I, Matthew Parker (1504–1575). Parker was a dutiful man and became archbishop under sufferance, keen to honour his queen yet wary of the damaging rifts in the Anglican Church at that time. The story goes that Parker did have a rather prominent nose, and as archbishop he carried out many inquiries into the actions of his clergy, leading many to consider him a busybody. The problem with this explanation is that there is no textual evidence for the use of the term before 1890; indeed, prior to the early nineteenth century the word 'nosy' just meant someone with a large nose (the Duke of Wellington, for example, was nicknamed 'Old Nosey' due to his oversized hooter). So who is the eponymous nosy parker? Lexicographers have noted that most of the earliest references to the term use 'Mr Nosy Parker', which indicates that it derived from an actual person. Hence the evidence to suggest anyone other than Matthew Parker has yet to be uncovered.

PALLADIAN *a British style of architecture based on classical designs*

Palladianism became popular in Britain between about 1715 and 1760. It is the style of architecture in which some of the nation's most famous stately homes of the era, such as Chiswick House in London and Holkham Hall in Norfolk, are designed. The movement is based on the designs of Renaissance architect Andrea Palladio (1508–1580), who himself harked back to ancient Roman styles, using strict rules of proportion to create plain but classical exteriors. Palladian designers such as Lord Burlington (1694–1753) were inspired by Palladio's designs and aped the style to create a uniquely British take on classical architecture, with clean, symmetrical exteriors but contrastingly sumptuous interiors.

PANIC *uncontrollable fear and anxiety*

Pan is the Greek god of the wild, shepherds and hunting. Hedonistic in character, Pan has the legs and horns of a goat, rather like a faun, and enjoys pursuing nymphs and playing on his pan pipes. The eponym 'panic' derives from Pan's powerful voice, which he used to cause sudden, contagious fear in people and animals alike.

PAPARAZZI *intrusive press photographers who snap celebrities*

The plural 'paparazzi', used to describe the hordes of voracious photographers who follow celebrities, derives from a character named Paparazzo in Federico Fellini's 1960 film *La Dolce Vita*. In the film Paparazzo is played by Walter Santesso, who accompanies Marcello Mastroianni's jaded hack Marcello as he travels through Rome in search of a good story. Due to the invasive nature of the packs of photographers snapping and buzzing about their celebrity prey, as portrayed in the film, it has been suggested that Fellini took the name from the Sicilian word *papataceo* for a large mosquito. The film was warmly received by the critics, winning the Palme d'Or at Cannes, ensuring it gained an international release and catapulting a new word into our language to describe the emergent tribe of intrusive photographers.

PASTEURIZE *to expose foodstuffs to high temperatures to kill off microbes*

Louis Pasteur (1822–1895) is today known as the father of microbiology for his achievements in developing germ theory – a concept which led to important advances in medical science and public health. Pasteur grew up in the Jura region of France, taking an early interest in art and science. By 1848 he had gained a post working at the University of Strasbourg and made his first major discovery: noting that molecules produced by living things were always left-handed, an important step forwards in our burgeoning understanding of microbiology. Pasteur went on to work at the University of Lille. In 1856 he began investigating why a local brewer's alcoholic drinks were souring. Pasteur's observations of the fermentation process led him to notice that food or drink went off due to contamination by microbes in the air – a revolutionary theory. Prior to this, decay was thought to be a spontaneous occurrence. It followed that 'germ theory', as it became known, contributed to the development of vaccines and inspired Joseph Lister (see page 70) to develop antiseptics. In 1863 Emperor Napoleon III asked Pasteur to save the French wine industry, which had been beset by sour wine. Pasteur conducted a series of experiments and discovered that heating the wine to 55°C killed the bacteria which turned it sour without ruining the taste of the wine. This process, which became known as pasteurization, not only saved the French wine industry but was later applied to milk and numerous other foodstuffs, preventing many deaths by keeping food free from germs.

PAVLOVA *a pudding made from meringue, fruit and whipped cream*

Anna Pavlova (1881–1931) was one of the first ballet superstars. Born in Russia to a washerwoman, Pavlova had a lowly start in life and yet she overcame her meagre beginnings through talent and hard work. Anna first saw a ballet performance when she was 8 – *Sleeping Beauty* at the Mariinsky Theatre in St Petersburg. She was immediately transfixed and decided that ballet was her future. Pavlova secured a place at St Petersburg Imperial Ballet School, where her natural ability and strong work ethic marked her out. On graduating she went straight into a ballet company and immediately began to make her name, her nuanced performance of *The Dying Swan* gaining numerous plaudits and becoming something of a signature role. Pavlova was soon named prima ballerina. She began touring the world with the Ballets Russes and then from 1911 with her own ballet company, making her one of the first truly global ballet stars. During one of her ballet tours to Australia and New Zealand in the 1920s a meringue and fruit dessert was created in her honour. The exact origin is unclear as many chefs have claimed to have been responsible for the pudding. However, what is clear is that by the mid-1930s in both Australia and New Zealand meringue cakes were being given the name 'pavlova'.

PENNSYLVANIA *one of the thirteen founding states of the USA*

The American state of Pennsylvania was established in 1681 after a royal charter was granted to William Penn (1644–1718). The state was named by Charles II in honour of William Penn's father, Admiral Sir William Penn (1621–1670), a royalist, who had remained loyal to Charles during Oliver Cromwell's rule as Lord Protector. When Charles II was restored to the throne, Penn was knighted and created a commissioner of the navy. Penn's son William was a Quaker and advocate of freedom of religion. Sir William Penn was initially unimpressed by his son's religious ideals, especially after he was expelled from Oxford on account of them, but in later life the two were reconciled. Penn was imprisoned a number of times for his Quaker publications, and he wrote his most famous work, *No Cross, No Crown* (1669), while imprisoned in the Tower of London. Facing constant religious persecution and the threat of prison, Penn sought to create a Quaker haven in the new colonies of America. He was granted a huge area of land between Lord Baltimore's province of Maryland and the Duke of York's province of New York by Charles II in lieu of a large debt Charles owed to Penn's father. William Penn established Pennsylvania with religious freedom as a central tenet and was instrumental in signing a successful peace treaty with the local Native Americans, ensuring the early colony flourished.

PETRI DISH *shallow glass dish for culturing bacteria*

Every student of biology will be familiar with petri dishes, the small, round, shallow glass plates used to culture bacteria. The dish was invented by German bacteriologist Julius R. Petri (1852–1921) while he worked as assistant to Nobel prizewinning scientist Robert Koch at the Imperial Health Office in Berlin. The team had recently been working on culturing bacteria on agar, a jelly-like substance derived from algae, an innovation suggested by Angelina Hesse, and in 1887 Petri went on to design and make the new glass dishes in which to better perform their experiments. The shallow petri dishes made growing and identifying bacterial strains much simpler and the tight-fitting lid kept the samples sterile. This extremely practical piece of equipment was also easy to slide under a microscope in order to examine the resultant microorganism. This simple yet effective piece of medical equipment has been instrumental in many scientific discoveries and is still widely used today.

PLATONIC *love that is not sexual*

Plato (*c*.428–347 BCE) was an Athenian philosopher whose influential dialogues have helped lay the foundations of modern Western thought. Plato was a student of Socrates and teacher to Aristotle – all key figures in the Ancient Greek world. The word 'platonic' comes from Plato's writings on the nature of love, which he outlined in the *Symposium*. The work is in the form of a dialogue with Socrates in which he discusses different types of love, from the fleeting earthly love rooted in sexual desire to the kind of love which transcends sexual feeling and takes us closer to the divine. It was this notion that during the Renaissance was taken up and associated with the non-sexual love felt between friends. Playright William Davenant is thought to have penned the first published use of the word in this context in the English language, in 1636. However, the concept is believed to have been in widespread use at this time.

PLIMSOLL LINE *a line drawn on the hull of a ship to mark the level of submersion the ship should not pass when loaded with cargo*

Samuel Plimsoll (1824–1898) rose from a poor childhood to become an MP. He campaigned tirelessly for better safety measures for seaman. One of the issues that most concerned

Plimsoll was the overloading of vessels by unscrupulous merchants, a lack of regulation which resulted in numerous ships losing buoyancy and sinking with the loss of many lives. In 1873 Plimsoll published *Our Seaman* in which he attacked 'coffin ships' – vessels that were overloaded and unseaworthy. His writings caught the public mood, and by 1876 the Merchant Shipping Act had come into force; this gave the Board of Trade rigorous inspection rights and introduced the Plimsoll line, a fixed loading line named in his honour which was painted on the hull of every British ship. The Plimsoll line ensured that inspectors could readily see that a ship full of cargo was not too low in the water. Plimsoll continued campaigning on issues of safety at sea for the rest of his life. He is remembered in his home town of Bristol, where a swing bridge on the Cumberland Basin was named Plimsoll Bridge in his memory. Today all cargo ships globally must have a Plimsoll line (also known as a waterline); the level is determined by a board of classification and the mark must be permanent so it cannot become illegible. Incidentally, the canvas and rubber **PLIMSOLL SHOE** also gained its name from the Plimsoll line: the thick rubber band around the shoe resembles the line on a boat's hull, and, like the line on boat, if water enters over the top whatever is inside gets wet – in this case the foot.

PLINIAN ERUPTION *the most violent of volcanic eruptions, which sends plumes of volcanic ash over 20 km into the air*

After the death of his father, Pliny the Younger (*c.*61–112 CE) was brought up by his uncle, the famous writer and scholar Pliny the Elder. Pliny the Younger worked as a Roman official and writer, his letters providing an important source of Roman history. In 79 CE Pliny the Younger watched from across the Bay of Naples as Mount Vesuvius erupted, killing his uncle and thousands of others in Pompeii and Herculaneum. He wrote two letters to the famed Roman historian Tacitus, in which he described the eruption with surprising objectivity, noting that the eruption column was shaped like an Italian pine tree. As a result of his accurate description of the catastrophic eruption, the most powerful type of volcanic eruption – of which Vesuvius was the classic example – was named Plinian in his honour. Plinian eruptions are rare and only occur once or twice every decade. Other famous Plinian eruptions include Mount Tambora in 1815 and Krakatoa in 1883, both in Indonesia. More recent examples include Mount St Helens, USA, in 1980 and Mount Pinatubo, Philippines, in 1991.

POINSETTIA *plant with red and green foliage, popular as a Christmas houseplant*

The poinsettia is native to southern Mexico. The Aztecs knew it as *cuetlaxochitl*, using the latex sap as a cure for fevers and the bright red leaves to concoct a red/purple dye. The plant was first noted by Europeans in the sixteenth century when Spanish explorers arrived on the continent, but the first samples were not taken until 1804 when explorer Alexander von Humboldt sent specimens back to botanist Carl Willdenow at the Berlin Botanical Garden. In 1834 the plant was given the scientific name *Euphorbia pulcherrima*, meaning 'most beautiful'. The common name, poinsettia, derives from Joel Roberts Poinsett (1779–1851), the United

States' first ambassador to Mexico 1825–29, and later in 1840 a founding member of the precursor to the Smithsonian, the National Institution for the Promotion of Science. Poinsett was a keen amateur botanist and collected plants wherever he went. In 1828 he sent the first live samples of poinsettia to his greenhouses in South Carolina, where he propagated it, sending the resultant plants to friends and family throughout the United States. One of the recipients was nurseryman Colonel Robert Carr, who immediately saw the potential in the colourful plant and in 1829 began cultivating and selling it through his nurseries. In 1836, historian William Prescott proposed the name 'poinsettia' in his book *The Conquest of Mexico,* in which he recounted the tale of Poinsett's role in bringing the plant to popular notice. Robert Graham created the genus *Poinsettia* to accommodate the plant (*Poinsettia pulcherrima* is now considered a synonym of *E. pulcherrima*). In the 1920s the Ecke family of southern California began growing fields of poinsettia and marketing them as a Christmas bloom, beginning the association of this plant with Christmas festivities. In 2002 Congress decided to make 12 December – the day of Joel Poinsett's death in 1851 – National Poinsettia Day to celebrate his life and the plant he made famous.

POMPADOUR *bouffant hairstyle*

This enduring hairstyle was named in honour of Jeanne-Antoinette Poisson, marquise de Pompadour (1721–1764), aka Madame Pompadour, patron of the arts and mistress to Louis XV. Poisson was a bright child; she was educated in art and literature, growing into a sparkling and intelligent young lady. She made a good marriage to Charles-Guillaume Le Normant d'Étioles and made a name for herself in society, becoming friends with luminaries such as Voltaire and Diderot. Poisson soon caught the eye of the king, Louis XV, who made her his mistress in 1745, securing her a legal separation from her husband and gifting her the title Marquise de Pompadour. Pompadour moved into Versailles and acted as private secretary to the king, becoming a vital part of the French court. Together with the king, Pompadour was a powerful advocate for the arts and together they commissioned many iconic buildings (such as the Place Louis XV, now known as the Place de la Concorde, and the Château du Bellevue) and promoted many artists and artisans, marking a golden age for the decorative arts in France. As Pompadour was a prominent taste-maker, her fashions were followed closely, including that of her bouffant hairstyle, which came to be known by her name. After a five-year love affair, Pompadour and the king ended their romantic liaison; however, she stayed on in Versailles, remaining a key advisor and confidante until her death in 1764.

PRALINE *sweet snack of nuts (most commonly almonds) boiled in sugar*

The origin of the name for this sweet snack is thought to derive from César de Choiseul, comte du Plessis-Praslin (1598–1675), whose chef, Clement Jaluzot, was said to have invented it. César was from a noble family from the Champagne region of France. He was a successful military leader and rose to become a Marshal of France, leading many victorious battles for King Louis XIV. César was said to have a delicate stomach and so to improve his health his chef invented the snack of almonds caramelized in sugar, which was named 'prasline' after his title, Maréchal du Plessis-Praslin. When Jaluzot retired from serving the Marshal he set up a confectionary shop in Montargis to sell his 'praslines'; from there their popularity grew and the name morphed into today's 'praline'.

PYRRHIC VICTORY *a victory which takes such a huge toll on the victors that it almost amounts to a defeat*

Pyrrhus (*c.* 319–272 BCE) was king of Epirus (modern-day north-western Greece and southern Albania), becoming king at the age of just 12. Pyrrhus was a well-respected military commander who fought in many wars. In his memoirs he wrote about the art of war, his wisdom later celebrated and quoted by revered ancient writers such as Cicero, preserving his voice. The term 'Pyrrhic victory' derives from two heavy battles he fought against the Romans: the Battle of Heraclea in 280 BCE and the Battle of Asculum in 279 BCE. In each case although Pyrrhus won the battle, his army sustained so many casualties that his forces were left depleted and unable to mount any further action, effectively annulling the victory. His accounts of the battles, quoted in Plutarch's *The Life of Pyrrhus*, sum up the situation neatly: 'If we are victorious in one more battle with the Romans, we shall be utterly ruined.'

RAFFLESIA *rare parasitic plant, native to South East Asia, with the largest flower in the world*

The Rafflesia is a remarkable plant: it contains no chlorophyll, so unlike most plants it cannot photosynthesize; instead it lives as a parasite on the Tetrastigma vine. After a number of years the plant produces its flower – the largest in the plant-world at over a metre in diameter – which gives off a putrid stench in order to attract carrion flies for pollination. The plant, native to the rainforests of Indonesia, is highly endangered. *Rafflesia* was discovered in 1818 by Sir Stamford Raffles (1781–1826) and Dr James Arnold – the genus *Rafflesia* was named after Raffles and the species *Rafflesia arnoldii* after Arnold. Raffles was a self-taught natural history buff, who joined the East India Company at a young age in order to support his mother and sisters. Raffles rose high in the company, wresting temporary control of Java, Indonesia, from the Dutch and later establishing the island of Singapore as a free port. Raffles spent a great deal of time in Indonesia and Malaysia, immersing himself in the culture and exploring the flora and fauna. When he returned to England he helped establish London Zoo. Today his collection of objects can be seen at the British Museum and his papers and books at the British Library.

RICHTER SCALE *a scale to measure the magnitude of earthquakes*

The Richter scale was developed by American seismologist Charles F. Richter (1900–1985) in 1935 in order to provide a method to measure the magnitude of an earthquake. Richter's work at California Institute of Technology (Caltech) in collaboration with Beno Gutenberg focused on measuring the strength of the ground vibration caused by the quake. This allowed seismologists to compare the severity of earthquakes as they occurred. The advantages of Richter's scale were that the mathematics involved meant that the seismograph did not have to be especially close to the quake for a reading to be taken, and the single-digit logarithmic scale made it easy to understand – a quake with a reading of 3 is relatively harmless, a reading of 6 would cause widespread damage and a reading of 9 or more would be catastrophic. Today scientists tend to use the more accurate moment magnitude scale (MMS), which was developed in 1979 to record the strength of earthquakes. However, the more familiar Richter scale is still widely used in the reporting of earthquakes in the media.

RITZY *very fancy*

César Ritz (1850–1918) was a Swiss hotelier who founded a number of now world-famous hotels, such as the Hôtel Ritz in Paris and the Ritz Hotel in London. Ritz was the youngest of thirteen children born into a poor family in Niederwald, Switzerland. At the age of 15 he was apprenticed as a sommelier in a local hotel, but was sacked after being told he would never make it in the hotel business, a slight that perhaps spurred him on to his later success. Ritz moved to Paris and worked his way up from waiter to hotel manager, steadily learning his trade and carefully noting the needs and likes of the high-class customers. Ritz became one of the first proponents of the idea that 'the customer is always right' and this maxim served him well, building his reputation as one of the most elegant and attentive hoteliers. In 1889 Ritz became the manager of the Savoy in London and employed the famed chef Auguste Escoffier, starting a long partnership. Between them they made the Savoy one of the most successful and glamorous hotels in London. In 1896 Ritz created the Ritz Hotel Syndicate with millionaire Alfred Beit and began opening his luxury Ritz hotels across the globe, with the Hôtel Ritz in Paris opening in 1898 and the London Ritz in 1906. Ritz's hotels, and therefore his name, became synonymous with luxury, and derivations such as 'ritzy' were being used to describe anything fancy and exclusive. The word was fully embraced by the English language after Irving Berlin penned the catchy song 'Puttin' on the Ritz' in 1929.

ROSS SEA   *a deep bay in the Southern Ocean off Antarctica*

James Clark Ross (1800–1862) first entered the navy at the age of just 11 and undertook his first expedition in search of the Northwest Passage in the care of his uncle, Sir John Ross, in 1818. Ross went on to take part in a number of Arctic voyages, becoming part of the team that identified the Magnetic North Pole in the far north of Canada in 1831. By 1839 Ross had been promoted to captain and he went on to lead what became known as the Ross expedition to Antarctica. This epic four-year voyage in the reinforced ships HMS *Terror* and HMS *Erebus* was instrumental in the exploration of Antarctica and saw many landmarks named by Ross, including the volcanoes he named Mount Erebus and Mount Terror, the Great Ice Barrier (later renamed the Ross Ice Shelf in his honour) and the Ross Sea. Ross's achievements in exploration were so great that he was post-humously honoured in the naming of a variety of other places and animals associated with the poles, including the James Ross Strait, Ross Point and Rossoya in the Arctic; the Antarctic Ross seal, Ross's gull and the Ross Dependency and Ross Island in the Antarctic.

SADISM *sexual pleasure from acts of cruelty*

The word 'sadism' was coined alongside 'masochism' (see page 77) in 1896 by German psychiatrist Richard von Krafft-Ebing (1840–1902). In his influential work on sexual patholo-gies *Psychopathia sexualis* Krafft-Ebing chose to name the trait of sexual cruelty after that libertine, philosopher and rake, the Marquis de Sade. Donatien Alphonse François, Comte de Sade (1740–1814) was most notable for exploring in his writings the darkest recesses of the human mind – causing scandal and leading to his repeated imprisonment for sexual crimes. In the notorious *120 Days of Sodom* (which was banned in his native France until 1957) de Sade extols the joys of all manner of sexual deviances from incest to paedophilia, which unsurprisingly made his name a byword for perver-sion. Although some modern scholars have attempted to rehabilitate de Sade as a great thinker, much of his work revels so deeply in the capacity for evil of the human condi-tion that it invokes revulsion rather than respect.

SALMONELLA *bacterial genus that causes food poisoning*

The genus *Salmonella* covers a whole host of diseases, many of which cause serious food poisoning. The most notorious member of the salmonella family is typhoid, responsible for many deaths, caused by faeces-contaminated water, which was first noted in 1873 by English doctor William Budd. In 1885 pathologist Theobald Smith first noticed the salmonella bacterium was present in pigs that had hog cholera, or swine fever. However, it was named after his boss (as was customary), the director of the Bureau of Animal Industry Daniel E. Salmon (1850–1914). Salmon was not entirely undeserving of this honour: in 1876 he became the first person in America to gain a doctorate in veterinary medicine; he went on to work in public health, attempting to identify the causes of many of the pernicious contagious diseases caught by farm animals in America. In 1892 Salmon set up the National Veterinary College in Washington DC. He served as president of the American Veterinary Medical Association. Ultimately Salmon performed vital research which showed the link between animal and human diseases. We shouldn't feel too bad for Theobald Smith: although he didn't get salmonella named after him, he did receive widespread fame as a result of his work identifying ticks as the cause of the spread of Texas fever in cattle, which led to the later discovery that insects were vectors in the spread of certain diseases, such as malaria and yellow fever.

SANDWICH *portable food, with a filling between two slices of bread*

Although John Montagu, the 4th Earl of Sandwich (1718–1792), probably did not invent this now indispensable style of food, it is almost certain he popularized it. Montagu was a keen gambler, spending hours at the gambling table in his club. Not wanting to interrupt the flow of play, Montagu would request that his servants bring him some meat inside two slices of bread, which he would consume whilst continuing with his game – the bread acted as a barrier that prevented his hands (and therefore his cards) getting greasy from the meat filling. It is thought that Montagu's fellow gamblers were most impressed by his portable snack and were soon requesting 'the same as Sandwich', inevitably leading to the natty new dining trend adopting his name.

SAXOPHONE *brass woodwind instrument*

Antoine-Joseph 'Adolphe' Sax (1814–1894) was a Belgian instrument maker who in the 1840s invented the saxophone. Sax had grown up playing the clarinet and flute, becoming proficient at both, but it was the mechanics of the instruments that really interested him. Sax's parents were both instrument makers and he too went into the business, intending to develop a new woodwind instrument but one made of brass, which he hoped would span the gap between the brass and woodwind sections in military bands. On 28 June 1846 Sax was granted a patent for his saxophone; he had designed a full range of the instruments from sopranino to contrabass. The saxophone was immediately embraced by military bands but the instrument failed to make any headway into classical orchestras. Sax continued to develop new instruments and enjoyed recognition as a master instrument maker. However, he was twice forced into bankruptcy and would die in poverty. The saxophone remained a fringe instrument until the 1920s when its dulcet tones were the perfect match for the growing jazz scene in America – at last the saxophone had found its niche.

SCOVILLE SCALE *scale to measure the heat of a chilli pepper*

Wilbur L. Scoville (1865–1942) was an American pharmacist who developed the 'Scoville Organoleptic Test' in 1912 while working for the Parke-Davis pharmaceutical company. The test measures the levels of the chemical compound capsaicin, which is what makes the heat in chilli peppers. Scoville's test works by giving each pepper a rating based on the amount of sugar water needed to dilute an extract of the chilli until it no longer has any heat – a level decided by a panel of usually five tasters. The test became standardized as the Scoville scale, with the unit SHU (Scoville Heat Units) indicating the degree of dilution required. For example, a Scotch bonnet pepper's score of 350,000 SHU means that one cup of the chilli would need to be diluted in 350,000 cups of water to make the heat no longer detectable. Despite its subjective nature the Scoville scale is still widely used today, alongside the more accurate high-performance liquid chromatography (HPLC) measure of capsaicin levels. To put the scale in perspective, an ordinary red bell pepper has a score of 0 SHU, the mild jalapeño pepper rates between 2,500 and 5,000 SHU, but the world's hottest pepper, the Carolina Reaper rates an astonishing 2.2 million SHU.

SEATTLE *city on the west coast of the United States in Washington State*

Seattle is one of the few major US settlements named after a Native American chief. Archaeological evidence suggests that Native American tribes roamed the Seattle area up to 4,000 years before the first arrival of European settlers in 1851. Arthur A. Denny led the European settlers, who became known as the Denny Party, setting up the first trading post in what is today Olympia. In 1852 local and well-respected Native American chief Si'ahl (rendered as Seattle in English) asked that the trading post be moved to Duwumps, the site of modern-day Seattle. As a result the store was named 'The Seattle Exchange' in the chief's honour, and from here the name came to represent the growing settlement. Chief Seattle headed the Duwamish and Suqwamish tribes. In 1852 he was baptised as a Roman Catholic. Seattle formed many friendships with the settlers and signed a treaty giving Europeans rights to the land in exchange for health care and education for the local tribes. Unfortunately the settlers did not stick to their promises and took the land, moving the tribes into overcrowded and disease-ridden reservations, and reneged on their agreement to provide support to the native population. Despite many other Native American tribes rising up against the settlers, Chief Seattle remained friendly and never fought them. When he died in 1866 many people of different races attended his funeral. In 1890 some of the original pioneers, including Arthur Denny, erected a memorial to the great chief at his grave site.

SEQUOIA *giant redwood tree, native to California*

The giant redwoods of California first came to scientific notice in the late 1840s and 1850s as a consequence of the gold rush. These imposing trees were named *Sequoia sempervirens* by Austrian botanist Stephan Endlicher – it has been presumed but not proven that he named the new genus after the famed Cherokee leader Sequoyah. Born between

1760 and 1765, Sequoyah (who also had the English name George Gist) had a Cherokee mother and a half-Cherokee, half-German father. Sequoyah worked as a fur trader. He became fascinated by Americans' ability to read and write. He began to believe it was the lack of written communication that was holding back the Cherokee and he determined to create a Cherokee writing system. With the help of his daughter Ayoka he began breaking the language down into syllable sounds and forming a system of symbols to represent the sounds. After twelve years of intense work, Sequoyah had developed a Cherokee alphabet. In 1821 he presented his system to tribal elders. Within just a few years many Cherokee had learned to read and write, and by 1827 a Cherokee-language newspaper was established. Sequoyah worked on as a diplomat for his people until his death. He was a celebrated leader and innovator in his lifetime, so it is unsurprising that his name was linked to the majestic new genus of trees. The story does not end there. In the 1850s, as European exploration of the Sierra Nevada area continued, a further species of giant redwood was identified. Samples were sent to England, where celebrated botanist John Lindley wrote a scientific description of the tree and named it *Wellingtonia*. When news reached America that this impressive American tree had been named after a British general the Americans were outraged. A diplomatic incident broke out, which was only calmed when Frenchman Joseph Decaisne pointed out that this giant tree was in fact clearly of the same genus as the newly discovered *Sequoia sempervirens*. Thus *Wellingtonia* became *Sequoia gigantean* (now *Sequoiadendron giganteum*) and the botanical tiff was defused.

SHRAPNEL *exploded fragments from the metal cases of artillery*

Henry Shrapnel (1761–1842) was a British officer who served in the army all over the world, in a lifelong military career. Shrapnel, a keen inventor, spent over twenty-eight years perfecting his design for the exploding shell. In the eighteenth century the solid cannon ball had been the most commonly used type of long-range ammunition. Shrapnel thought he could better the design by creating a hollow shell, filled with small metal balls, with its own fuse and gunpowder, meaning the shell would explode over the enemy, showering them with metal and causing maximum damage. The British Army adopted Shrapnel's invention in 1803 and it was used to devastating effect during the war against the French and at the 1815 Battle of Waterloo. Shrapnel shells were used right up until the beginning of World War II, when they were superseded by new highly explosive ammunition. However, the word 'shrapnel' was retained to describe the exploded metal from shell casings, which continued to wreak havoc on the battlefield.

SIDEBURNS *facial hair at the sides of the head, in front of the ear*

What we today call sideburns have been part of men's facial furniture for centuries, but were known by other terms, such as mutton chops or side whiskers. Sideburns did not get their eponymous name until the 1870s, inspired by the popular (yet unsuccessful) American general and politician Ambrose E. Burnside (1824–1881), who sported prominent mutton-chop whiskers which segued into a lavish moustache, leaving his chin bare. This memorable look caught the public imagination and – despite his military failures during the Civil War – people soon began to refer to this style as 'burnsides' in his honour. As with many word origins, over time it was modified: no one is sure why but by 1875 the elements had become transposed to produce 'sideburns'. It is possible that this version of the word persisted because the hair concerned is on the side of the face. The alternative word 'sideboards' (with board meaning edge or border) also has currency.

SILHOUETTE *a picture made from a black paper cut-out portrait of the sitter as if in shadow*

We can be sure that silhouette pictures are named after Étienne de Silhouette (1709–1767), who was finance minister under King Louis XV, but the derivation is obscure. One theory is that Silhouette's name became a byword for a miser, after his unsuccessful tenure as finance minister during the Seven Years War. Silhouette attempted to impose some austerity on the profligate French court, not least the closing of loopholes which allowed the richest to escape paying their taxes. Unsurprisingly this was unpopular among the aristocracy and he was soon sacked. As a consequence his name became associated with penny-pinching; it has been suggested that it was for this reason that the cheap shadow portraits which became fashionable during this period were known by his name. Other historians have put forward the theory that Silhouette was himself a big fan of the shadow portraits and had many hanging on the walls of his château.

SPOONERISM *an error when the speaker inadvertently transposes the initial letters of two or more words*

Everyone's done it: 'fighting a liar' instead of 'lighting a fire'; 'a blushing crow' instead of 'a crushing blow'; 'a half-warmed fish' instead of 'a half-formed wish'. The Reverend William Spooner (1844–1930), lecturer at New College, Oxford, was so liable to verbal accidents that his name became indelibly associated with them. Spooner was an albino and as such his eyesight was very poor, which perhaps half-explains his errors. He was also said to be extremely intelligent, with his mind working so fast it was often far ahead of his mouth. Clearly fondly remembered, his Spoonerisms (and many other apocryphal ones) have gone down in history, such as this gem which he supposedly uttered to an especially lazy student: 'You have tasted a whole worm' (wasted a whole term). A similar spoken gaffe is the **MALAPROPISM**, whereby a similar sounding word is used incorrectly (and often humorously) in the place of the correct term. Malapropisms are named after the character Mrs Malaprop in Richard Brinsley Sheridan's play *The Rivals* (1775).

STETSON *the most famous type of cowboy hat*

John B. Stetson (1830–1906) was born in New Jersey to a hatter father. After contracting tuberculosis he travelled out West for his health. While camping out in the open, Stetson fashioned himself a hat from beaver hide. It had a wide brim and a tall crown, which helped keep the head warm and dry. Legend has it that he initially wore it as a joke and was ridiculed for his strange-looking headgear, but as time went on the practicality of the hat became apparent and he saw its potential when a fellow cowboy swapped him a gold nugget worth $5 for the hat. Stetson travelled back east to Philadelphia, Pennsylvania, where he set up a hat-making business, manufacturing sturdy outdoor hats based on his time in the West. His most popular design was for 'the Boss of the Plains', or 'the Boss' for short, which he began making in 1865. It had a flat brim with straight-sided crown and hatband. The Boss was an expensive hat, but proved so practical that it became extremely popular with ranchers in the West, who would steam and shape the hat themselves, creating the familiar creases in the crown we know today. The Stetson soon became the hat to be seen in. Famous faces of the Wild West, such as Annie Oakley and Buffalo Bill, were fans, making the name Stetson synonymous with the cowboy hat.

STONEWALL   *to obstruct someone or be evasive*

In 1861 'stonewall' was given as a nickname to Confederate general Thomas J. Jackson (1824–1863), one of the South's most successful leaders during the American Civil War (1861–65). At the First Battle of Bull Run, Jackson was reported to have stood firm like a literal 'stone wall' – and the nickname, which seemed to sum up the fortitude of Jackson, stuck. By the 1880s the word began to creep into common usage to mean obstructive behaviour, especially in Parliament, where it became used as a synonym for filibuster.

STROGANOFF *beef dish cooked in mustard and sour cream*

A classic beef stroganoff recipe is strips of beef tossed in mustard and finished off with sour cream – a marriage of French and Russian cuisine which reflects its origins. It is thought the dish is named after Russian diplomat Count Pavel Stroganov (1774–1817), for whom the recipe was created by his French chef. The Stroganovs were an old Russian family of great wealth, and Count Stroganov would have circulated in the highest echelons of society, spreading the popularity of the new dish. Beef Stroganoff was first published as a recipe in the 1871 edition of *A Gift to Young Housewives* by Elena Molokhovets, cementing the dish's relationship with the prominent Russian family. It became popular in Britain in the 1930s after it first appeared in *Good Food* by Ambrose Heath, and by the 1970s was a dinner party staple. A slightly different version of the dish (based on canned mushroom soup and tomato ketchup) developed in the United States after the recipe arrived via post-Revolution Russian exiles living in China. The Chinese served the dish over rice and it was this iteration which arrived in America in the 1940s.

SVENGALI *a person who wields hypnotic or excessive control over another*

In 1894 George Du Maurier's novel *Trilby* was published. Set in bohemian Paris of the 1850s, it tells the story of a young French girl, Trilby O'Ferrall, who is completely tone-deaf, and yet when the mysterious Hungarian Svengali takes her under his wing she rises to great success as a singer. Svengali (a character subsequently criticized for anti-Semitic undertones) uses his powers of hypnosis to enchant Trilby and send her into a trance in which she can perform beautifully. Ultimately Svengali suffers a heart attack and is unable to hypnotize his protégée to perform. She breaks free of his influence but is humiliated by her sudden lack of singing talent, and in typical Victorian fashion she soon dies a tragic death. *Trilby* was published serially in *Harper's Monthly* and was sensationally popular. It was later made into a stage play in which the lead character sported a hat; this became known as a **TRILBY** and has persisted in popularity. The dark character of Svengali caught the public imagination and entered into the lexicon to describe a man who exercises control over and exploits a young protégée.

SYPHILIS *an especially nasty venereal disease*

Debate rages over whether the disease syphilis originated in the New World or the Old World, but what is clear is that by the sixteenth century it was making its presence felt across Europe. Some historians argue that it was Christopher Columbus and his crew who brought the disease back from Hispaniola (modern-day Haiti and the Dominican Republic). An alternative theory suggests the disease was always present in Europe but was not recognized as an illness distinct from leprosy, which has similar symptoms, until the 1500s. Due to the virulence of the disease it was generally named after national enemies, so in Britain it was known as the French Disease, the French called it the Neapolitan Disease, and so on. In 1530 a renowned Italian physician and poet, Girolamo Fracastoro (1478–1553), wrote the poem *Syphilis, sive Morbus Gallicus* (Syphilis, or the French Disease), in which the title character is a shepherd called Syphilis, who after insulting the sun god became the first person to be struck down with the dreaded disease. Fracastoro continued working on an early precursor to germ theory (some 300 years before Louis Pasteur; see page 90) and in his influential 1546 treatise *De Contagione et Contagiosis Morbis* referred to the disease by the name he invented, 'syphilis'. This caused it to be taken up by doctors and researchers (although, of course, colloquially the disease was still frequently named after national foes).

TANTALIZE *to torment with something desirable and yet unobtainable*

This eponym derives from the Greek myth of the sorry character Tantalus, who suffered an agonizing eternal punishment. Tantalus was initially an intimate of the gods of Olympus and was frequently invited to dine with Zeus himself. However, he proved himself unworthy of this favour when he was found to have stolen some ambrosia from Mount Olympus in order to impress his friends. Tantalus tried to make up for his mistake by inviting all the gods to dinner, but on realizing he was short on food he inexplicably decided to kill and cook his own son, Pelops. The gods refused to eat, except for Demeter, who ate Pelops' shoulder. At this point the truth came out. A furious Zeus restored Pelops to life (minus his missing shoulder, for which he substituted an ivory replacement). Zeus' anger with Tantalus could not be assuaged by his apologies and he was handed down a cruel eternal punishment: he was destined to stand forever in a pool of water, but every time he bent down to drink to satisfy his raging thirst the waters would recede. As well as this he was also plagued by a constant hunger, and yet if he reached for the delicious and ripe low-hanging fruit ranged around the pool the branches would forever prove to be just beyond his grasp.

TASMANIA *a large island state off the south coast of Australia*

Tasmania was first sighted by a European on 24 November 1642, when Dutch explorer Abel Tasman (*c.*1603–1659) named it 'Anthony Van Diemen's Land' after the governor of the Dutch East Indies. Tasman was a very successful explorer. From about 1632 he worked for the Dutch East India Company and began exploring the seas of the southern hemisphere. During his most successful mission, in 1642, Tasman discovered Tasmania, New Zealand, Fiji and Tonga, and circumnavigated the Australian continent but without actually spotting land, leaving James Cook to 'officially' discover it in 1770. It was not until the early 1800s that the British set up a colony in Van Diemen's Land, establishing it as a penal colony with 308 convicts in 1803. Thousands of convicts were sent to the island, which devastated the natural landscape and sparked a war with the native Aborigines, who were entirely wiped out or relocated by 1838, in what many historians have rightly called a genocide. To escape this difficult past and separate itself from the history of the penal colony, Van Diemen's Land was in 1856 renamed Tasmania in honour of Abel Tasman.

TAWDRY *cheap, tacky, gaudy and of poor quality*

In 679 CE Etheldrida (who later became known as St Audrey), daughter of the king of East Anglia, died from a tumour in her neck. The Venerable Bede, writing in *The Ecclesiastical History of the English People* in 731, reported that she was likely struck by the affliction from which she died because she frequently wore many showy necklaces. St Audrey became the patron saint of fenland Ely; each year on her saint's day of 17 October a fair was held in the city, known as St Audrey's Fair. At the fair many cheap, poorly made items would be on sale, including bands of silk lace or ribbon, which were worn around the throat in memory of the patron saint and became known as 'Saint Audrey's laces'. This gradually became contracted and corrupted to (by the end of the sixteenth century) 'taudrey lace' and then to 'tawdry', which became synonymous with cheap, tacky goods.

TEDDY BEAR *a stuffed toy bear*

In November 1902 American president and keen huntsman Theodore Roosevelt was on a hunting trip in Mississippi. His companions clubbed a bear, tied it to a tree and invited Roosevelt to take a shot, but he declined, stating that it was unsportsmanlike. The press soon picked up on this incident and cartoonist Clifford Berryman drew a popular depiction of the scene in the *Washington Post*. Brooklyn shopkeeper Morris Michtom and his wife Rose were inspired by the cartoon and created a fabric bear in honour of President Roosevelt and placed it in their window display with a sign reading 'Teddy's bear'. The homage captured the public imagination and the Michtoms began manufacturing teddy bears and other soft toys to meet demand. The popularity of the toy bears and their association with Teddy Roosevelt were sealed when German seamstress Margarete Steiff began her own line of lifelike mohair bears. The bears were first shown at a toy fair in Germany in 1903, where they were seen by an American toy company, which placed a large order, stoking the craze for the toy bear in America. It soon became one of the most popular stuffed-animal brands in the world. In 1906 the name of the Steiff bears was officially changed to 'teddy bears', absorbing the presidential association and ensuring the name stuck.

THESPIAN *an actor*

Thespis was a Greek poet and playwright active in the sixth century BCE. Unfortunately none of his plays has survived. Ancient sources suggest Thespis was the first recorded actor of a Greek drama and the inventor of Greek tragedy. Aristotle provides evidence that Thespis changed drama forever when he emerged from the chorus to act alone on the stage. This innovation saw Greek tragedies being performed by a single actor, changing masks to portray numerous characters and backed by the traditional chorus – it was not until the fifth century BCE that playwright Aeschylus began writing plays with two actors and a chorus. The word 'thespian' to describe an actor first came into use in the late seventeenth century.

TITIAN *hair of a golden-red hue*

Titian (Tiziano Vecellio) was born in Venice *c.*1490. He became one of the most important painters of the Venetian school. Unlike many painters both before and after him, Titian's brilliance was recognized in his lifetime. He had a number of international clients, including Holy Roman Emperor Charles V. Titian painted portraits as well as religious and mythological scenes; among his most famous works are *Bacchus and Ariadne* (1522–23), *Venus of Urbino* (1534) and *Danaë with Nursemaid* (1553–54). Titian frequently painted women with flowing golden-red locks. From the nineteenth century his name began to be used to favourably describe redheads, which was a departure as red hair had formerly been perceived as unattractive and undesirable.

TOURETTE'S SYNDROME *a neurological condition in which a person is affected by involuntary physical and verbal tics*

Georges Gilles de la Tourette (1857–1904) was a colour-ful character who provoked both admiration and ridicule during his lifetime. He trained as a doctor, specializing in hysteria and hypnotism; today he would be recognized as a neurologist, a label that did not then exist. In 1884, as part of his medical work, Tourette described in a medical paper nine patients with a mental condition that presented in verbal and physical tics, the first time such a condition had been formally recognized. Despite receiving positive recognition for his medical work, Tourette became infamous for an unfortunate series of events. In 1893 a former patient, Rose Kamper, burst into his consulting rooms and shot him in the head, causing superficial injuries. Kamper claimed that Tourette had hypnotized her against her will, causing her to become mentally unstable. Tourette strongly refuted her claims and refused to accept that hypnotism could be inflicted on someone without their consent. Nevertheless a debate raged in the press over whether hypnotism could be used to turn an ordinarily law-abiding citizen into a criminal. The furore had a profound effect on Tourette, who became depressed and manic in equal measure – at times suicidal, at others appearing as the star speaker at literary talks he had organized. Ultimately his mental health suffered to such a degree that around 1902 he lost his professional post. Soon after he was tricked into being admitted into an asylum in Lucerne when a colleague told him a patient was desperate to see him. Gilles de la Tourette never left the asylum and died a few years later.

VOLT *unit of electric potential*

Alessandro Volta (1745–1827) was an Italian physicist who invented the electric battery. Volta began experimenting with electricity while he worked as a physics teacher, and soon his research led him to isolate methane for the first time. As his knowledge grew, Volta began to travel around Europe performing his experiments with electricity and sharing ideas with other prominent scientists of the day. In recognition of his work he was made a fellow of the Royal Society in 1791, and in 1794 he was awarded the Copley Medal for his contribution to the understanding of electricity. Luigi Galvani (see page 52) announced his 'discovery' of animal electricity in 1791; Volta, fascinated by this line of research, began duplicating the experiments. Volta, however, concluded that it was not the animal that was creating the electricity but rather two different metals in contact. This breakthrough led Volta to continue his research in the field, which ultimately resulted in the voltaic pile battery: alternate discs of copper and zinc stacked between pieces of cardboard soaked in brine. This development represented a great leap forward as it was the first electric battery able to continuously provide an electric current to a circuit. In 1801 Volta demonstrated his battery to Napoleon, who was so impressed that he made Volta a count and a senator of the kingdom of Lombardy. In 1881 it was decided that the SI unit to measure electric potential should be named the volt, in recognition of Volta's enormous contribution to electrical science.

WELLINGTON BOOT *a calf-length leather or rubber boot*

Up until the early 1800s most British soldiers wore 'Hessian' boots – calfskin leather boots, cut high to the knee with a deep V to the front and tassels. However, the new fashion for wearing tight-fitting linen breeches did not work well with this style of boot and so Arthur Wellesley, the future Duke of Wellington (1769–1852), asked his shoemaker, Mr George Hoby of St James's Street, London, to make him a new style of boot. Made from highly polished calfskin leather, the new boots had no tassel and were cut at mid-calf, making them comfortable and practical for riding. Wellington was a great military commander; after he sported the boots during his decisive victory in the Peninsular War at the Battle of Vittoria in 1813, the new style, now known as 'Wellingtons', became the height of fashion for soldiers and civilians alike – a status further cemented by his subsequent victory over Napoleon at Waterloo in 1815. Wellington went on to become prime minister in 1828 and he remained an extremely popular and heroic figure until his death in 1852. In 1856 the Scottish North British Rubber Company began manufacturing the first vulcanized rubber gum boots. These rubber boots were very close in cut and style to Wellington's famous boots and the company began marketing the gum boots as Wellingtons, to capitalize on the duke's enduring reputation. Rubber wellies exploded in popularity during World War I, when thousands of pairs were manufactured for the soldiers serving in the trenches. After the war the multiple uses for the practical waterproof boots were recognized and they soon became favourites with farmers and gardeners alike.

WISTERIA *woody stemmed climber with distinctive flower cascades*

American anatomist and physician Caspar Wistar (1761–1818) was honoured in the naming of the plant genus *Wisteria*. Wistar was a scientific intellectual who held frequent salons at his home in Philadelphia, where numerous notable bright minds gathered to discuss ideas. His gatherings became known as Wistar Parties. They continued to be held regularly after his death. One of Wistar's most notable legacies to science was his article on the anatomy of fossils, which he wrote in 1797 after his friend Thomas Jefferson announced the discovery of the fossilized remains of a large quadruped, which he named *Megalonyx* (giant claw). Jefferson suggested that the fossil represented a large cat-like beast, but Wistar examined the anatomy of the bones and posited instead that it was more likely to have represented a giant sloth-like creature, an assertion which would later prove to be correct. The first wisterias to reach Europe were collected by Mark Catesby in Carolina in 1724. It was initially known as *Glycine frutescens*, or colloquially as 'Carolina kidney bean' because its spotty seeds were thought to resemble tiny kidney beans. Chinese and Japanese wisterias came to Europe via collectors for the East India Company in 1815; they are today the more common and popular varieties. It was Thomas Nuttall (1786–1859), an English botanist who spent most of his life working in America, who chose the name 'wisteria', reflecting his admiration for the noted Caspar Wistar. The anomalous spelling has caused some confusion over the years, with some botanists insisting on using 'wistaria' to more properly reflect the plant's origin. However, Nuttall himself always used the spelling 'wisteria' and so, according to the rules of botanical nomenclature, this original spelling must persist.

FURTHER READING

Auchter, Dorothy, *Dictionary of Historical Allusions and Eponyms*, Oxford, 1998.

Beeching, C.L., *A Dictionary of Eponyms*, 3rd edn, London, 1968.

Columbia Lippincott Gazetteer of the World, Columbia NY, 1952.

Davies, J.L. (ed.), *Atlas of Tasmania*, Hobart, 1965.

Everett-Heath, J., *Concise Dictionary of World Place-Names*, Oxford, 2014.

Fritze, Ronald, *New Worlds: The Great Voyages of Discovery 1400–1600*, Stroud, 2002.

Freeman, Morton S., *A New Dictionary of Eponyms*, Oxford, 1997.

Goetzmann, W., and G. Williams, *The Atlas of North American Exploration*, New York, 1992.

Henderson, G.D., *3000 Plus: The Original Munro Map*, Haddington, 2013.

Knight, Franklin W., and Henry Louis Gates (eds), *Dictionary of Caribbean and Afro-Latin American Biography*, Oxford, 2016.

Letusé La O, Rogelio A., *Elsevier's Dictionary of Eponyms*, London, 2001.

Manser, Martin, *Chambers Dictionary of Eponyms*, Edinburgh, 2004.

Safier, Neil, *Measuring the New World: Enlightenment Science and South America*, Chicago, 2008.

Scholl, Andrew, *The Achilles to Zeppelin of Eponyms*, London, 2000.

Woodham, Jonathan M. (ed.), *A Dictionary of Modern Design*, Oxford, 2016.

INDEX OF EPONYMS

INDEX OF NAMES